Simplified Organization

LEARN TO LOVE WHAT MUST BE DONE

Mystie Winckler

Simplified Organization: Learn to Love What Must Be Done

Paperback: 978-1-7374517-3-0
Audiobook: 978-1-7374517-4-7
Ebook: 978-1-7374517-5-4

First paperback edition: November 2023

Edited by Harmony Harkema
Publishing and Design Services by Melinda Martin
Photo by Jordan Edens Photography

To

Stefani Mons

and

Leisa Moulton

Who have made this material their own
and improved it in the process.
Thank you for helping me keep
Convivial Circle running.

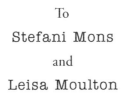

Download the free companion checklist at

SimplifiedOrganization.com.

Cease endlessly striving
for what you want to do
and learn to love
what must be done.
—Goethe

Contents

Contents

Introduction

> The business done in the home is nothing less than the shaping of the bodies and souls of humanity.
>
> —G. K. Chesterton

I am living the life I always wanted. I grew up the oldest of seven, homeschooled, reading *Anne of Green Gables* and heaps of sappy Christian romance novels. I grew up with my mom in the home, always, even though it meant some extremely lean times. I saw and understood that my parents believed raising children was more important than growing bank accounts. My siblings and I were more desirable than money.

It was obvious to me as a child that having my mom at home was better than driving a nice car or eating at restaurants. In my simplistic, childish worldview, it seemed like a dichotomy. You choose mom at home, or you choose stuff. I was glad my parents chose kids at home, and I preferred to be home with my mom and siblings even when it meant powdered milk.

As a child, it seemed clear to me that home and children was the best way to spend time and resources. When I grew up, I knew I'd make the same choice myself. Who would rather work a job than make and grow people? Who would prefer a paycheck over being in charge of a household? I never planned on doing anything else.

I married at nineteen and, after finishing college, moving back to our hometown, and getting health insurance through my husband's first full-time job, we happily began our family. I knew how to cook. I knew how to load the dishwasher. I could do laundry. Homemaking was going to be a piece of cake, right? There isn't much to it, really, and you get the perks of being in charge!

Expecting homemaking to be comprised mostly of menial tasks, I put my energy not into doing those menial tasks with skill, but in figuring out the best way to set up systems that would minimize the amount of time I spent on them instead. Even after a childhood with a stay-at-home mom, many household chores, and practice cooking, I still disdained housework. Even with my conservative family priorities, I thought managing a household required a minimum of effort.

Modern society conditions us to assume a homemaker's work is mundane, outsourceable, unfulfilling work. Even if we choose it, even if we value it, we still underestimate homemaking. We wake up one day, surprised to find that it is a lot of work—turns out we're wholly unprepared for all it demands of us.

In America, you go to college so you can get a better job. But homemaking is one of those jobs—like barista or retail clerk, not like teacher or engineer—anyone can learn by doing, no degree required. On the one hand, we believe homemaking is meaningful work, yet on the other hand, we don't think it takes any real training, education, or skill.

Past societies didn't rely on colleges to train for occupations. They used apprenticeships and relational training. Children learned how to work from their parents. Tradesmen learned their craft from an experienced master. Knowledge and skills were passed along via relationships over time.

But today's homemaker-mom is generally alone with her small children, with no one there helping her see the next thing she ought to do. Who will help her sort out the details and make it all fit into a manageable whole? We can blame our mothers, but our mothers likely didn't have mothers who taught them, either.

Homemakers might not be professionals, but we still need training, skills, growth, and encouragement in our valuable work. I grew up in a home with a homeschooling, stay-at-home mom; I am the oldest of seven children. I did at least know how to change diapers, how to direct toddlers, and how to cook a few meals for a crowd.

I helped with chores. I knew what family life was like. I expected to be able to walk into my own role as mom, ready to nail it. Despite my early systems, despite my best-laid plans and good intentions, I did not nail it.

A couple of years ago, someone left a comment on a blog post I wrote about teaching kids to do chores. "It doesn't take years," he wrote, "to train kids how to do something any adult can learn in five minutes." Here is one problem we discover as homemakers: we have no idea what it even looks like to respect our own occupation because our culture does not respect it.

In that blog comment, I recognized my own trouble as a young wife and mother. I had accepted the belief that homemaking was just a collection of menial tasks—the kind of thing that, yes, anyone could learn in five minutes. So why was I having such a hard time? Simply because homemaking is *not* something anyone can learn to do in five minutes.

Our unseen disrespect for homemaking as a vocation affects even those of us who choose it. We see it when we hanker after titles like Domestic Engineer or Chief Operations Officer. Such titles imply that homemaking is inferior and needs some beefing up for the resumé. We see it when we discuss how much a mom would earn if she were paid for her various tasks. Such calculations defend homemaking while falling prey to the assumption that everything ought to have a monetary value attached to it.

Before economies or politics can even exist, there must be people. People made in the image of God need no additional decoration to make them respectable. People made in the image of God do need homes and families—and that's exactly what we provide as wives and mothers. Our work is good, valuable work, no matter the time period, governmental structure, economic type, class, or culture we are in.

The work of homemaking is of utmost value to culture and society, whether or not that culture and society values it. Even if a woman has another job—one that earns her money—her most significant contribution to her family and to the good of the nation and world is her homemaking.

Homes, after all, shape people. Those people, in turn, shape the culture, society, nation, and world into the next generations.

Let's not be surprised when that level of influence demands difficult, time-consuming work.

Why We Want to Get Organized

When I was first trying to figure out the very best, most strategically clever homemaking methods, my goal was to earn the "organized" status and, ever after, have life flow smoothly and easily. I assumed organization was something I would set up once, and then I'd be ready to rock and roll. Instead, I would set something up, halfheartedly work my system for awhile, then I'd either get bored and disregard my system or some life-shakeup—like a new baby or a move—would occur, and I'd be knocked back to square one, or so it felt.

If we're honest with ourselves, we keep trying to get organized because we feel that if only we could accomplish that, then the unexpected would never happen, we'd never be unhappy, we'd achieve perfection. However, organization cannot do that for us. It is a false hope for salvation or perfection. If you're like I was in my twenties, this sounds like a discouragement from getting organized, but it's only a reality check.

Even if it's not the amazing solution to all our problems, organization is worth pursuing. When we organize our stuff and ourselves, we are imitating God. God made the world deliberately in an ordered, structured manner. He makes promises and keeps them. He keeps track of all His purposes and all His people. He wants our corporate worship of Him to be done decently and in good order. As beloved children, we mimic our Father's providential care in our own derivative way.

We get frustrated with organization when we unconsciously think we're achieving not reflective imitation, but rather precise, god-like control. We are to be like Jesus by following after Him, loving what He loves, hating what He hates, and obeying all He says. We imitate, but we do not compete. We are not to strive to be god in our life. God Himself exercises providential care and control, and our care and attention only dimly reflect Him. Our plans do not work out as we expect, but God's plans always work out, and our plans are not His plans.

> Being organized is being prepared and ready for whatever comes from God's fatherly hand.

Being organized isn't about being in control, always having your ideas for your home and life and family work out. Instead, being organized is being prepared and ready for whatever comes from God's fatherly hand.

Why Getting Organized Is So Hard

When we're not organized, we feel life's pressures, and we want to crawl under the covers to avoid the day before us.

When we're not organized, instead of being prepared, we aren't sure what's next, we don't know what's for dinner, and we misplace things like our car keys. Instead of knowing where things belong, we set them down absent-mindedly. We end up with random piles all over the place, and we can't find what we need when we need it, which is part of being prepared. Instead of knowing our commitments and responsibilities, we have a vague, nebulous sense of what we "ought" to be doing, as well as a sense of guilt and obligation that we can't nail down.

When we feel frustrated and defeated, as if we're banging our heads against a wall, it's usually because our reality doesn't line up with our expectations—and one expectation might be simply that homemaking shouldn't take much of our time and attention.

Becoming an organized, capable, confident homemaker is a worthy goal, and one that will take years, not a day or two, to master. For me, it took at least ten years. However, it took ten because of the stubborn years I spent denying that my messy habits and poor management practices were a problem. I didn't need a hack or some new secret sauce. I needed a kick in the pants. God knew what I needed when I did not and sent that kick in the pants through many means.

I enjoy reading productivity books, and I've tried applying their various principles to homemaking. Here and there, this practice has been helpful, but only after I stopped thinking my job was to be amazing and started walking humbly before my God. One kick-in-the-pants source in my life has been the articles, books, and workshops of Rachel Jankovic.

In the first chapter of *Loving the Little Years*, she started with: "There is only one thing in my entire life that must be organized. The kids can be running like a bunch of banshees through a house that appears to be at the bottom of a toaster, and yet, if organization and order can still be found in my attitude, we are doing well."

I read that, stunned. I realized all my attempts at organization were aimed at my material circumstances rather than my heart and attitude. I needed to organize my attitude before I would get any traction in organizing my home.

My whole life since has been a testimony to this truth. It is the way God made and runs the world. In this book, I'll share many stories from my struggle years, stories from my attempts at solving my problems myself, and what I learned really needed to happen. For nearly the first decade of my marriage, I worked at systems and organization not because I loved homemaking, but because I wanted to find any and every clever hack to get me out of the work. I wanted the homemaking equivalent of a get-rich-quick scheme.

> My hope is that this book will help you skip the angst of avoiding the work so you can cut to the chase and learn to love what must be done because the work is good work.

Such attempts never worked. What *did* work was dedicating myself to the calling of faithfulness in the midst of an ever-changing life for the long haul. My hope is that this book will help you skip the angst of avoiding the work so you can cut to the chase and learn to love what must be done because the work is good work.

I believe God is calling women out of the feminist lie that we are not fulfilled by homemaking and into the glorious truth that we can love the work and dance within the rhythms of life. We have a lot of baggage to drop on our way out of postmodernity. The good news is that scrubbing toilets, making grocery lists, and washing sheets all work for our rehabilitation into the glories of confident womanhood.

Our effectiveness in the world at large as women begins when we are effective in our homes, because homes are where people start, land, and connect. There is no greater privilege than to be given a home to run. We can and should glory in our duty as we learn the ropes of doing it faithfully.

There is no greater privilege than to be given a home to run. We can and should glory in our duty as we learn the ropes of doing it faithfully.

For we are his workmanship, created in Jesus Christ for good works, which God prepared beforehand, that we should walk in them.

—Ephesians 2:10

PART 1

Understanding Our Situation

Father, I know that all my life is portioned out for me;
the changes that are sure to come I do not fear to see:
I ask thee for a present mind, intent on pleasing Thee.

I would not have the restless will that hurries to and fro,
seeking for some great thing to do or secret thing to know;
I would be treated as a child, and guided where to go.

Wherever in the world I am, in whatso'er estate,
I have a fellowship with hearts to keep and cultivate;
And a work of lowly love to do for the Lord on whom I wait.

I ask Thee for the daily strength, to none that ask denied,
a mind to blend with outward life, while keeping at Thy side,
content to fill a little space, if Thou be glorified.

In service which Thy will appoints there are no bonds for me;
my secret heart is taught the truth that makes thy children free;
a life of self-renouncing love is one of liberty.

Anna Letitia Waring, 1850

1

Why Am I Overwhelmed?

Even when everything is crazy, you can be calm and enjoy your life

There is always time to do the will of God. If we are too busy to do that, we are too busy.

—Elisabeth Elliot, *Secure in the Everlasting Arms*

I remember sitting on the couch in the living room one afternoon. Large with child, I was enjoying the quiet house while my eighteen-month-old napped. We took a walk after an early lunch. I had started a load of laundry in the morning, and it was waiting for me to move it to the dryer, yet I sat.

My toddler had played with the pots and pans, which were still scattered across the kitchen. I wasn't sure what I was going to do for dinner. It had been at least two weeks since I'd cleaned the bathrooms—maybe more. There was an unlimited amount of housework I *could* do—vacuum, mop, dust, clean out the fridge, wash the sheets. All of these things were probably overdue. Still, none of them were a visible problem—yet—so why bother?

I kept reading my novel on the couch. I was sluggish. I was uninspired. Everything could wait until I felt like doing it. After all, when I felt like doing things, I could start a cleaning frenzy and get a lot done in a short burst. Plugging away and just doing a little at a time seemed inefficient.

Suddenly, I realized it was four o'clock. The baby's nap had been unprecedentedly long. My husband would be home in half an hour. I saw the house with new eyes. Feeling the time crunch, I quickly made a dinner plan while also whipping the kitchen back into shape. My husband wouldn't mind that things weren't tidy, but I didn't want it to look like I hadn't been doing anything all day. It was the panic-clean of a guilty conscience.

By the time my husband walked through the door, I was slightly out of breath from my tidying sprint, and the house looked like I had things in hand—except for the fact that I hadn't been downstairs to move the laundry. In the end, I'd be washing that load again because it sat in the washing machine too long. The afternoon frenzy was necessary to mask the reality—to myself as well as my spouse—that I was being irresponsible.

Getting Out of Your Head

I'm sure I'm not the only one who has stood in the middle of the house, paralyzed and staring. Everywhere I looked, there was a task screaming for my attention. Every room needed to be decluttered, cleaned, and organized. I felt like not a single thing was the way it was supposed to be.

My to-do list had become so long that I had no idea where to start. And that was just the *written* to-do list. The mental to-do list, swirling in my head, was even longer. It left me swamped by a sense of impending doom. There was no such thing as catching up. I had zero chance of knowing—much less doing—all the things I ought to have been.

If you find yourself in a similar place, with multiple responsibilities, each involving many duties—some urgent, some important, some unlisted and possibly even unknown—it's natural to feel overwhelmed. But take heart. There is hope. You're not stuck.

You can get on top of your home routines and your life management duties. However, it will take more than an hour, more than a day, and getting on top of it will look different than an Instagram post on organization might lead you to believe.

We all feel pulled in a million directions at times. Parenting, cooking, cleaning, laundry, errands, church, and activities all add to our plate and take time in our day. However, we must remember that good work is supposed to take our time and our energy. Our time and our energy are gifts given to us to be invested in God's kingdom for His glory.

Our time and our energy are gifts given to us to be invested in God's kingdom for His glory.

Obligations to others are opportunities for service, not impositions. We are given time and energy not to hoard them or dole them out in miserly pinches. The whole point of having time and energy is to spend them on others in service to God for His glory. They are just some of the talents (*see Matt. 25:14–30*) God has given us in this life that we are to return to Him with a profit.

Unwittingly, the way we respond to the demands on our time and resources contributes to feeling overwhelmed and perpetuates an unhealthy stress response when none is necessary. The tidying-up whirlwind I described above was a common pattern for me. The only kind of cleaning I knew was frenzied activity. Cleaning took tons of energy, so I didn't feel up to it most of the time, but the energy I thought I needed was adrenaline-driven rather than the steadiness of well-paced self-management.

When our expectations and experiences equate getting the housework done with an adrenaline-driven frenzy, we can interpret being overwhelmed as a method of motivation. We move from feeling swamped by a flood of responsibilities into a frantic agitation as we quickly check off as many items on our to-do list as we can. We must find new paths to motivation.

It's Your Mind That's Overwhelmed

There are no perfect routines we can put in place that will enable us to never feel overwhelmed again. Circumstances sometimes collide and collude to send us into a crazy-making mental spiral. The best solution is not to seek out systems that will bring immunity to overwhelm, but rather to learn standard tactics for managing our response when life seems unmanageable.

Being overwhelmed by normal life responsibilities is a personal response, often one that becomes a default, a habit. It is not an objective fact, not an outward reality. Rather, "overwhelming" describes our thoughts and emotions about a situation. We can respond differently. We don't have to be overwhelmed.

One way to handle a flooding mental spiral is to sit down and declutter the most chaotic place of all: your head. To declutter your head, you need to do a brain dump. A brain dump is simply writing down everything that pops into your thoughts. Write down whatever is on your mind—on paper—no matter how far-fetched or obvious those thoughts seem.

Once you see all the things that are vying for your attention, you'll immediately feel clearer and calmer because your mental energy will be freed from the burden of remembering details. When we're tracking so many details in our head, our thoughts feel jumbled and fragmented. We're unable to focus patiently, think creatively, or problem-solve logically.

As you brain dump, you'll be able to think through whatever issues come up rather than simply mentally rehashing the details. Writing will help you make connections and analyze a situation rather than feel overwhelmed by it. When you get all of your thoughts down on paper, you will

Writing will help you make connections and analyze a situation rather than feel overwhelmed by it.

often discover that the scattered craziness you felt was all in your head. With your thoughts visible in writing, you can analyze them without being overwhelmed by them.

When you're overwhelmed, your first impulse might be to ignore and avoid most of what's weighing on your mind. However, before you're able to focus, you have to clear your head and free your mind and emotions from the burden of holding vague obligations. Telling yourself, "I have too much to do!" or "I'm being pulled in a million directions!" are generalizations that make focus and attention impossible. They justify our fretfulness and worry.

Worry is best handled by prayer. Prayer is like a vacuum running over the crumbs of worry. Sometimes, after my kids vacuum, you can't tell they've done it. Most of the crumbs are still there. I call them back and remind them that they're not done until the crumbs are gone. It's the same with us, our prayers, and our worries. Prayer removes worry because it aligns our heart and mind with God's will for us. Noticing a worry means noticing a thing to pray about. A worry should not be a prompt to fret, but a prompt to pray.

> A worry should not be a prompt to fret, but a prompt to pray.

If we're overwhelmed, we may struggle to identify our specific worries. We may feel like we don't know what to pray for. Our hazy sense of innumerable pressures turns off our ability to think and to pray. We can clear our mind and pave the way for prayer through a brain dump.

Begin listing the seeming million things pulling at you, one at a time.

As you name them, they will lose their grip on you. Instead of feeling like your many vague, strangling emotions are driving, *you* take the driver's seat by getting specific and writing things down, praying through your thoughts as you go.

Try it. It works.

There's (Not) Too Much to Do!

When we feel overwhelmed, we tend to assume we must be trying to do too much. Our mind is whirling with tasks and projects that we can't keep straight. Everywhere we look, we see more to do, more we haven't been doing, more we *could* do if we weren't already so behind.

When we feel like we're drowning, it's natural to want to fix the problem by cutting back. The problem, we *think*, is the work itself. Change the routines, change the expectations, change the load, and then we'll be able to handle it. However, when we start with the situation instead of with ourselves, we're usually blame-shifting. Finding an external fix can be a way of avoiding an honest self-examination.

Cutting back when we're drowning is like draining the pool until we're standing. Perhaps we're no longer drowning, but we also aren't swimming. We've changed the game instead of learning the game. Instead of working to increase our strength, stamina, and skill, we've stopped. People afraid of drowning in a pool need to take swimming lessons, not avoid pools.

Let's be honest. What we find overwhelming is usually the work involved in our basic responsibilities, not the things we can reasonably cut from our life. The problem isn't that the duties exist; the problem is that we don't know how to manage them effectively.

Cutting back without self-reflection won't make us feel better. We haven't improved when we've cut back. We haven't matured. We've only asked our responsibilities to scale back to a more comfortable level when we could be allowing them to stretch us to new levels of growth.

Elisabeth Elliot wrote, "The secret is Christ in me, not me in a different set of circumstances." We look around our home, and we know we have a problem. We want our circumstances rather than ourselves to be the problem. We think that if we can fix our circumstances, we'll be golden. Instead of beginning with our circumstances, though, we need to begin with ourselves and our relationship to God.

Feeling overwhelmed isn't necessarily an indication that we have too much to do. Our first response should be to pray and give our cares to Christ. When we realize we can't handle our own life, we don't have to panic; instead, we can rest in our dependence on our loving and faithful God. Feeling overwhelmed is a reminder that we can't do our life in our

> Feeling overwhelmed is a reminder that we can't do our life in our own power, so we need to stop and ask Christ to give us clarity and wisdom, joy and strength.

own power, so we need to stop and ask Christ to give us clarity and wisdom, joy and strength.

If we cut back to only what we can do on our own, without Christ, we will be limiting God's calling on our life. Our impulse to keep things within the bounds we can control is an impulse to be the servant burying his talent in the ground because life seems too risky. God calls us to do much with what He has given us, promising us wisdom and the fruit of His Spirit as we do what appears to be impossible—even if the thing that seems impossible is simply feeding everyone a meal on time and then doing the dishes.

I have found that when I feel like there is too much to do, I am usually wrong. I am catastrophizing. I am being a drama llama. I am avoiding. So instead of allowing my feelings to stall out and remove me from the game, I use them as a cue to simply start with the easiest, most obvious task, which is usually a chore that causes internal revolt. Just take out the garbage, even though someone else should have done it. Just wash the dishes, even though the stacks are intimidating. It's amazing how little time it takes for a huge heap of dirty dishes to become a heap of clean dishes when I get down to business without procrastinating and complaining.

Doing one small job is the fastest remedy I know to stop feeling like a failure. It gets me out of my head—where the chaos really is—and as I move and work, my thoughts can sort themselves out. Maybe I was overwhelmed by things I didn't really need to be doing or thinking about.

Accomplishing something, no matter how small and seemingly insignificant, is the real antidote.

Embrace Opportunities to Stretch

When the house is full of needy people, it's not always clear where to start. However, it *is* clear that God's will for us is to give thanks and grow in the fruit of the Spirit. Those needy people and the little emergencies placed in our days are the opportunities He's given us to grow in love, joy, peace, patience, kindness, goodness, faithfulness, gentleness, and self-control. These are God's will for us.

No matter what happens, we can orient ourselves to the interruptions, to the needs, to the emergencies by asking God to give us the grace to grow in fruitfulness through them. These aren't fruits that spring up spontaneously in our heart if we just wait long enough. They are fruits that the Spirit gives us when we ask for them through thankful prayer—and then work out what He has worked in.

> No matter what happens, we can orient ourselves to the interruptions, to the needs, to the emergencies by asking God to give us the grace to grow in fruitfulness through them.

Although feeling overwhelmed is a natural response, the Spirit gives us the ability to practice a *supernatural* response to every situation we find ourselves in. We are not left to ourselves. We have a playbook, and we have the Spirit to coach us. Sanctification is the process of the supernatural fruits of the Spirit becoming more and more natural to us as we ask God for them and willingly put them into practice as the need arises.

Every situation that feels overwhelming at first is just a practice play, a drill, sent by God. It's a chance to replace our instinct with His, to choose His way instead of our own way. When we recognize God's direct and personal hand in our life, we learn that our tension and angst is inappropriate.

Our fretfulness is replaced with curiosity about what God is doing now in and through us. Our spiraling negativity is replaced by gratitude for all the ways God has called us to serve. Our inner turmoil is replaced by a willingness to practice kindness and gentleness instead, stepping into the good work before us with humble joy. God's sanctification plan for our life consists of replacements like these.

There's Always Time to Do the Will of God

Over a dozen years after the scene recounted at the beginning of this chapter, I'd still look up with surprise when the clock struck four. With five kids instead of one, homeschooling half of them, teaching the others the basic habits of civilization, leading the church's women's ministry, and running a mini-business, my work patterns were almost unrecognizable.

I didn't have more time than I had when I was younger. In fact, I had less discretionary time. However, after years of intentional practice, I learned how to be more strategic with my time. Even more importantly, I learned how to operate from a joy-based mode rather than a stress-based mode.

The joy came from being in God's Word and building the habit of prayer. My thoughts didn't swirl into an unceasing, crazy-making spiral. I stopped having to write them down in order to pray about them. When I thought of all there was to do and I felt the panic and doubt start to pull me under, I could immediately tell God about it instead of attempting to work it out in my head.

After all, I had tried many times to work things out in my head, to sort the jumble and stop the swirl. It never worked. Prayer *did* work. God always gave me the peace with which He promised to guard my heart and mind in Christ Jesus when I asked Him for it. I learned I didn't have to know how everything was going to pan out in the end in order to take the next step—any step—of faithfulness.

God didn't need me to figure out life first. He wanted me to trust Him with my life and my work. He wanted me to rely on Him and not on myself. Now I almost laugh at myself when I feel a surge of overwhelming angst. A moment of panic has become a reminder that I have some things to give over to God, and I can be grateful for the reminder. My goal isn't to avoid feeling overwhelmed, but to do the right thing with that feeling: *pray*.

Over the years, I learned to pray and do the next thing without worrying about how "everything" would get done. The reality is that everything is never done. My job isn't to do everything on my list, but to take the next step of faithfulness where I am. That I can do—and so can you.

My goal isn't to avoid feeling overwhelmed, but to do the right thing with that feeling: *pray*.

Take a Baby Step to Beat Overwhelm

Set a timer for five minutes and do a brain dump. Then set a timer for another five minutes and pray about everything you just dumped onto paper.

> *I remind you to fan into flame the gift of God, which is in you through the laying on of my hands, for God gave us a spirit not of fear but of power and love and self-control.*
>
> —2 Timothy 1:6–7

2

What Is Perfectionism?

Perfection isn't our goal in this life.
Sanctification is.

It's better to do less than you hoped than to do nothing at all.

—James Clear, *Atomic Habits*

I thought I was being strategic, not perfectionistic. I never thought of myself as a perfectionist. After all, I didn't measure things when I cooked, and I kept my socks piled, unmatched, in a drawer. How could I be a perfectionist if I hated ironing and avoided folding the laundry?

I refused to make my bed, and I procrastinated as long as possible on dishes, but I spent hours outlining home systems that would make everything run on autopilot—that is, without my effort. Perfectionists were quilters and people with immaculate homes, I thought. My life and my home were so far from perfect that it was obvious I wasn't trying to be perfect, right?

Wrong. The reality was that I knew I couldn't be perfect, so I refused to try. I kept looking for the system that would require as little time and effort as possible because I didn't want to try too hard, much less look like I was trying hard and failing.

When I was thirty, my mom told me a story about my youngest sister, ending with "She's a perfectionist, just like you." *Blink. Blink. What?*

A perfectionist is exactly what I'm not, I thought.

My mom continued, "She won't hang up her clothes at all unless she reorganizes her closet and arranges everything by color while she's at it."

Oh. Is that weird? Is that perfectionism?

Around the same time, an online mentor of mine, Cindy Rollins, let drop a line of T. S. Eliot's poetry that hit home: "Dreaming of systems so perfect that no one will need to be good."

The truth was that I was living like a slob because I didn't want to *start* until I could guarantee a beautiful *finish.* I was spinning my wheels trying to invent a system that would keep the house running like a well-oiled machine without any effort. Until I discovered the optimally efficient way to do everything all at once and all together, I wasn't going to do *anything.*

My mom was right. I was a perfectionist.

Ugh. I Can't Figure This Out.

The goal of homemaking isn't a perfectly clean and put-together home. The goal is making our resources useful and available for building up people. This means that those large housework projects don't need to be complete in order for us to be faithful in our work. The room doesn't have to *stay* clean in order for cleaning it to be worth our time.

Perfectionism slows us down and prevents us from making real, meaningful progress. It paralyzes our organization attempts. We need strategies for beating perfectionism so we can organize life and get things done.

Perfectionism is the desire for an outcome to be perfect, to be 100 percent complete. If something is perfect, it's not only beautifully executed, it's also finished. A thing that is perfect has no need or capacity to change.

God is perfect, and He created us to be perfect. However, because we are sinful, we have fallen from our intended capacity for perfection. In spite of this, we still have a longing for perfection, and that longing is not wrong. It's a longing for God Himself, for everything to be as it was intended to be. When we attempt to satisfy that longing by our own efforts, however, we end up dissatisfied and even depressed. Try as we might, we will never be God.

When Jesus returns, He will glorify us and restore in us our perfected human nature. When we look at the big picture in light of this truth, perfection *is* the goal. However, perfection arrives only in Christ at the Second Coming. In this life, we experience progress through sanctification, not perfection. Through struggle, we grow in dependence on God by faith.

Our struggles aren't problems to fix. Do we really think we can find a way to not have to struggle anymore? Our struggles are opportunities to mature in Christ. By making us aware of our sin and weakness, He brings us to the point of repentance and dependence so we can receive His forgiveness and enjoy freedom and faith. Forgiven, we rejoice in grateful obedience, engaging in the good works God has prepared for us and living as a sacrifice of praise. Instead of looking for the perfect solution that will fix all our problems, we can rejoice in everything and walk in faithful obedience, right where we are.

Replace Perfectionism with Faithfulness

Perfectionism says we need to be fully in charge of every situation. We need to be completely capable of doing a job perfectly, of fulfilling a role excellently. When it becomes clear that this isn't possible, perfectionism says to cut back until we *are* fully in control. Perfectionism assumes a successful woman is completely in charge of her life, always calm, always competent, always able to handle whatever comes her way.

We aren't that on top of our life, though, are we? And when we're not, we think something is wrong. But what if we're just being challenged? If everything were always easy and under control, we'd stagnate. We would not actually be satisfied and happy. What if we are experiencing not failure, but a call to growth, maturity, change, and sanctification?

Of course, God is the one who defines success for our days, for our life, for our roles and responsibilities. We have to know and love His Word so we can align our definition of success, perfection, progress, and holiness with His. We are not called to be all that we need in and of ourselves because we can't. We aren't.

We are called to faithfulness, and part of faithfulness is recognizing that we are weak, incapable of handling everything that comes our way—yet we have a dependable, fully capable God who gives us the strength that we need, not necessarily to be the most awesome version of ourselves, but rather to be loving, faithful servants who are ready and willing and excited to see God be awesome in our lives.

To be dependent on God and to grow in sanctification—which Scripture says in several places is God's will for our life—is a calling we can be faithful to and successful in. Sanctification is growth in holiness, in love of God and neighbor. That doesn't look like success in the world's terms, but it does look like growth.

Growing our capacity for love and faithfulness is not necessarily doing all the things with calm awesomeness. It is being willing to take a humble, small step forward, regardless of the outcome. God is the One who will be awesome in our life, not us. He is in control of every situation in our life, and He is the strength and salvation and love that we need, come what may.

He is the strength and salvation and love that we need, come what may.

Every time we feel inadequate, we're in the right spot because that's the truth. We're not capable, but God is. We can rely on Him to work through our feeble efforts. God gives us good work, and then God uses that work for His own ends, which is His own glory and our sanctification. He does all things well.

Choosing the Iteration Strategy

We want housework to be something we can check off and be done with, but that's simply not its nature. We will never complete everything all at once. The fact that housework won't be done in this life need not discourage us. Instead, we can choose to practice, to make progress, and to give up on our false hopes of being "done."

Progress doesn't come after we've figured out the perfect system. Progress comes one step at a time, incrementally, over the long haul. A desire for completion is usually a desire for perfection. We need a strategy to replace our desire for perfectionism. I call this strategy *iteration*.

To iterate means to perform repeatedly, to repeat a procedure, applying the result of the previous application to the next one. It's technically a math term, but it applies beautifully to our busy life at home, which is so full of details and needs.

Iteration means that we take a few small steps forward, look back to assess and learn after each step, then take a few more small steps forward, incorporating what we learned so far. Instead of waiting for the ideal or jumping to the final goal, iteration looks for progress, then improves and adapts as progress is made. Rather than create all the routines, systems, or plans from scratch before beginning in an attempt to implement a flawless scheme from the get-go, we need to iterate.

Iteration is a technique used in computer programming because technology and user requirements can change so rapidly that a plan engineered from beginning to end is often not applicable by the time the project is complete. In order to respond to technological and market change, software developers work on key features, roll them out, then evaluate the next most important thing to do.

Likewise, mothers don't know how conditions will change within the year or decade; we, too, should work on iterations, not a perfect system engineered up front. We don't know when the toddler will give up naps and change the rhythm of our days. We don't know what opportunities will arise for our junior high kids.

Iterate. Don't wait until the plan is perfect. Just start with what you have, where you are. Start using your plan before it's perfect, and the next plan you make will be better still. Think of your new routine as the first attempt at an experiment you're going to learn from, not as a forever-solution to put in place.

Don't wait until the plan is perfect. Just start with what you have, where you are.

A routine you make after experimentation and reflection will be better, more applicable, more personal. By trying out an imperfect plan rather than waiting until you have everything just so, you discover what works for you and what doesn't. By iterating, your plans and systems can grow and adapt to fit your life as it unfolds.

Iteration looks at a goal and asks, "What is one step toward the goal that I can take right now?" Therefore, with iteration, we make incremental progress and learn along the way. We don't stall out by trying to skip straight to the goal from where we are in one big leap.

Try iterating on a project you've been. Dive in, each day, to the responsibilities in front of you. Don't let the perfect be the enemy of the good. Don't let perfectionism keep you from getting started.

Organizing My Closet

A decade after my mom's comment, I am still tempted, every time I do laundry, to procrastinate putting it away because my closet isn't the paragon of order I'd like. Every basket of clean laundry calls to me as an opportunity to pull everything out and try again from scratch. However, ever since my mom's comment, this impulse now makes me laugh at myself.

I laugh at my many attempts to buy closet organizers, different kinds of hangers, new sets of bins—at how I always thought that my next attempt would finally "work." But what does "work" even mean? The hangers aren't going to put away my clothes for me. The bins won't put themselves back together after my hunt for just the right outfit.

No matter what the size or arrangement of the closet, no matter what organizational tools I do or don't have,

I have to put away my clean laundry. I have to put away the clothes I've worn and will wear again, not dump them on the floor or bedroom chair.

When I put away my clean clothes and keep my things neat, I am organized. My clothes don't have to be meticulously arranged. They don't have to be in matching containers, folded like origami.

When I try to implement standards whose primary purpose is to make me look good, to give me a sense of control, to achieve some ideal, then it's inevitable: my closet descends into chaos, because I can't maintain perfection. Not only that, but I won't do the small thing that makes the most difference because I'm not counting that as "done" or "good enough."

Perfectionism leads to procrastination. In its desire for complete control, perfectionism, ironically, leads to chaos. The more we give into perfectionism, the more likely it is that—one way or another—our situation will devolve into greater and greater disorder.

Sure, sometimes I do need more hangers or different bins, but I no longer think a new bin is the secret sauce I've been missing which will at last bring me an idyllic closet. My laundry basket will still hang out too long at the foot of the bed until I mentally shake myself and get to it, without worrying about finishing it perfectly or arranging everything just so.

Take a Baby Step to Beat Perfectionism

Choose one small area of your house that bothers you or that you've been putting off. Set a timer for ten minutes and simply do what you can in that time, stopping when the timer goes off.

> *Rather, speaking the truth in love, we are to grow up in every way into him who is the head, into Christ, from whom the whole body, joined and held together by every joint with which it is equipped, when each part is working properly, makes the body grow so that it builds itself up in love.*
>
> —Ephesians 4:15–16

3

What Is Homemaking?

Homemaking is caring for people and their creaturely needs

> What you do in your house is worth as much as if you did it up in heaven for our Lord God. We should accustom ourselves to think of our position and work as sacred and well-pleasing to God, not on account of the position and work, but on account of the word and faith from which the obedience and the work flow.
>
> —Martin Luther

For the first six or so years of marriage, I hated housework. I was torn between wanting to be a good, competent homemaker and thinking that the state of my bedroom or the kitchen wasn't a big deal. I could get meals on the table, keep things stocked, and complete a project just fine. But day-in-and-day-out routine tasks were a drag.

I didn't want to change, either. Some people keep clean houses and like it and some people don't. *That's just the way it is, right?* Some people are readers and others aren't. Some people love math and others hate it. *I can just be one of those people who is mediocre at the drudge work. What's the problem with that?*

A light cracked through my hardhearted stubbornness when my thirdborn was just a baby, and I was reading novels. Often, our failure of motivation is a failure of imagination. *Mansfield Park* by Jane Austen was my first wake-up call, reorienting my sense of reality.

In the novel, the heroine returns from her privileged uncle's country home to her own family's dingy home near the port. There, the dishes are given a cursory swipe but not actually cleaned. *Oh, I do that with my cookie sheets and muffin tins.* The bedrooms are wrecks because nobody cares about the state of things. *Well, what's wrong with that?* Was I supposed to be annoyed by Fanny's manners, or was she the barometer, telling me what should be the norm?

Fanny was not unreasonable. I was. I thought that the cleanliness of a house didn't matter much—and it showed. Certainly, I believed my ready smile and quickness to forgive spoke volumes about my character, but I didn't believe the state of my laundry room did.

I wanted to disconnect my character from the way my character lived in space, but how I functioned was evidence of my character. The problem wasn't really the layer of grime in the laundry room or fridge or bathroom. The problem was that I was irresponsibly dropping the ball. The problem was that I thought the way I kept house didn't reflect upon the kind of person I was.

Another novel drove this idea home later that same year. As I listened to the audio version of *Bleak House* by Charles Dickens while I painted the kitchen, it dawned upon me that the integrity of the main character was established by the way she kept house. If she had not kept house the way she did, it wouldn't have been congruous with her integrity. *Wait. Whoa. What did that mean about the slipshod way I was keeping house?*

Maybe I'm Not Cut Out to Be a Homemaker

When I was a young mom, leaving as much housework undone as was feasible, I told myself that some people just liked to clean, and having a clean house mattered to them. I, however, didn't like to clean, and I didn't care if the house was clean or not. So the Cleanies could work out their preferences, and I could work out mine. No harm, no foul. You do you.

My goal was to spend the least amount of time possible cleaning. Not surprisingly, as I worked toward this goal, I discovered that simply not cleaning and not caring about the state of the house was the most effective way to spend less time cleaning. When I focused on minimizing effort and time rather than on any outward standard, lethargy became the inevitable conclusion because it is the epitome of minimal effort.

For several years, I became a studious practitioner of not caring. I could always whip things into shape in an afternoon or two if needed, so it didn't inhibit our hospitality much. In fact, I came to enjoy the caffeinated whirlwind approach to cleaning. It seemed boring to just keep the house in a decent state with regular routines.

Functioning in the boom-and-bust cycle of house cleaning became more than a haphazard approach or default setting. It was the strategy I intentionally chose. Because I had chosen and cultivated this approach, shifting gears was incredibly difficult when I became convicted that my attitude about housework was all wrong.

Our attitudes and our actions work together, demonstrating what we love and prioritize. To change one without changing the other will never result in long-term change. Like diet and exercise for weight loss, character development requires adjusting both attitude and action in tandem.

More than out minds, our heart leads our choices, whether we like it or not. Allowing ourselves to be led by our default emotions rarely produces love and fellowship. At the same time, ignoring our emotions doesn't make them go away. Ignoring our feelings is just another way of being held captive by them.

Ignoring our feelings is just another way of being held captive by them.

These are not the only two responses. Both blindly following and callously ignoring our emotions assumes we have no control over them. Historically, in classical and medieval thought, emotions were recognized as guides that must be trained, informed, directed. This process was called *ordo amoris*, ordering the loves.

We can change not only what we do, but how we feel about what we do, even housework. This is the work of organizing our attitude, our affections, our loves. As we do the work of homemaking, we can also begin reorienting our heart toward our home and the work it takes to make a house a home.

People Need Homes, So We Need Home-Makers

In the midst of laundry, dishes, messy floors, dust, and clutter, homemaking can seem like a daunting and thankless job. Children undo our work as soon as we do it, so what's the point? Our husband doesn't notice that we swept, so does he even care? No one offers cheerful, diligent help—us included.

Then there's the fact that our culture does not value homemaking unless it's a million-dollar remodeling show. TV houses and Instagram scenes are not representative of busy, active family life, but they are held up as the standard we're supposed to desire. They teach us—wrongly—that the point of homemaking is to express our personal taste.

When we let Scripture determine our mission, however, we realize that homemaking is a service we render to God and His people. Only with that purpose in view can we rejoice as stewards in the place God has put us. Homemaking is not about mastering cleaning lists and chores but about loving and serving people, making homes in which they—and we—can flourish.

Homemaking is a service we render to God and His people.

Biblical homemaking is not about achieving a certain look in the home. Homemaking is a service of love to those who live in and enter our home. That means that what TV, magazines, and social media call homemaking probably isn't. Homemaking isn't about decor or style or expressing ourselves.

A homemaker is one who does what it takes with what she has to make a home. She is a manager, running an organization: a life-giving home. All that we do as wives and mothers shapes others. *How* we do what we do also shapes others. Such is the responsibility and vocation of a homemaker.

Homemaking, as Edith Schaeffer reminds us, is an art. It's not merely a set of tasks; it's a vocation. It's a discipline, but a creative one. If homemaking is making a home "particularly as a pleasant place in which to live," as the dictionary says, then our first duty as homemakers is not to find the perfect schedule for chores, but to be pleasant ourselves.

What will make home more pleasant than having a cheerfully bustling wife and mother at its core? Of course, the floors should be scrubbed, the sheets washed, and the meals prepared—these are the works keeping our hands busy. But what makes us homemakers is our orientation and demeanor, not our tasks alone.

Women are designed with homes literally built in. Wombs are symbolic as well as real. Try as many people might, there is no denying the creation reality that women are made to multiply and nurture people. To strengthen and grow our family, we need to embrace the wonder and joy of being homemakers, in our very person as well as in our actions and environment.

As moms, we are the centrifugal force in the center of our family unit, furiously active, yet often hidden. Without the center pull of gravity we provide, everything spins out into chaos: home, people, society. However, our inner self alone does not create the pull that holds the family unit together; our actions and our work do as well. Our inner and outer selves working together where God has placed us produces a compelling, gospel-picturing family life.

Our inner and outer selves working together where God has placed us produces a compelling, gospel-picturing family life.

The Practice of Homemaking

Homemaking is the *action* of making a home. The goal of our homemaking is not achieving an aesthetic. For example, the purpose of making dinner is feeding people, not impressing people. If our primary objective is to make a meal, our living room, or our kitchen sink photo-worthy, we're acting like photography is our main gig. If our primary goal is keeping our home *just so*, then we're living as if we're home stagers rather than homemakers.

Now, homemakers are *not* glorified janitors, a class set apart to clean up the messes others make while those others do the important work. A homemaker's mission is to emulate Jesus, who is preparing a place for us, who has created and called a people for Himself, who wants so much to feast in fellowship with a great multitude of people that He died to take the punishment for their sins and reconcile them to His Father. Heavenly glory is a homemaker's vision. We work out small foretastes of Jesus's work for us, presenting them to our family—and anyone else in our home—for their nourishment.

As homemakers, our work is a practice, much like a doctor has a practice—work he repeats day in and day out, managing the well-being of the people in his care. If we need more skill in executing our routine tasks well, then it is helpful that they are so repetitive—we always have more opportunity to practice!

The only way to get better at something is to do it over and over again, and housekeeping inherently requires us to do the same things over and over again. Instead of seeing this repetitiveness as a drag, we can choose to see it as an opportunity. I can improve because I am going to be practicing.

We tend to see repetition as a problem because we're focused on being *done*. Our job as homemaker isn't to be done with the work; it is to continually hit the reset button. Everyone knows what the reset button does to a computer. Sometimes you just need to hit reset. It fixes a lot of the problems, right?

> Our job as homemaker isn't to be done with the work; it is to continually hit the reset button.

In the same way, doing the dishes, washing

the sheets, cleaning the bathrooms—all these are just reset buttons, and it's our job to make sure they each get pushed often enough that things continue running smoothly. The real point isn't that we finish washing the dishes; the point is that the dishes are ready for the next meal. They've been used, so we hit reset.

Homemaking Means Caring

If you're like me, you've probably longed for the days or the countries where household help was standard. Somehow, I always assume I'd be the one who has the help, not that I'd be the servant. Yet in every age, women have done the nitty-gritty work of making a home. Whether she does the work herself or outsources it to others—or to machines as we do now—the lady of the house oversees the operation of her home.

A homemaker may or may not be the one washing her sheets, but she ensures it is done. She may or may not be the one washing the dishes, but she sees to it that there are dishes, that they are clean, and that there is cause for using them (i.e., regular meals).

The duty of the homemaker is to take the resources of the family and distribute them as required to care for the family. A homemaker provides comfort and a base of operations not only for her family, but also for her community.

A homemaker's concern is to first make a home for her family, then to extend the joy and provision of that home out to where it is needed. We truncate the role of homemaker when we limit it to meals, laundry, scrubbing, and vacuuming.

Homemaking is not over when the kids are grown and gone because homemaking extends beyond our family and beyond our house. Whenever and wherever we nurture the development of others, care for the hurting, and bond people to one another and the greater body of Christ, we are working within an extended sphere of homemaking.

Assume a Business-Owner Mindset

A homemaker is important not only because someone has to change diapers and wash dishes, but because someone has to *care*—it is the homemaker's business to care for and about people. Every successful business is managed well; success is built upon someone making it his duty to oversee the processes and do what is needed to keep everyone and everything running well.

Every home is like a small company, a band of people outfitted for a mission. To be effective, this small company requires a manager. God cares about families being successful missions in the world, so he qualified one half of the human race to be operations managers of the home. We aren't homemakers because we have chosen this life. We are homemakers because God has called us to it and equipped us for the mission.

Often, viewing our work at home as a job is part of what makes us discouraged by it. A job is an arrangement whereby we do a set of tasks, and in return, we get compensation. Even schools are set up on a job model. Students do the work assigned by the teacher, and in return, they get a grade and a piece of paper that signals their preparedness for the next job.

Students don't have to care about the work; they just have to do it. Employees might like their work, but whether they do or not is irrelevant. What matters is checking the boxes and punching the time clock. Some people will like their jobs and others won't, but everyone who wants a paycheck has to do their job.

So when it comes to managing a home, we flounder. There is no time clock, no hourly rate, no company-imposed checklist. There are no deadlines; there are no paychecks. All the affirmations and credit we're used to are gone. No wonder we struggle. However, being a homemaker is so much better than being an employee. We just have to approach it with a business-owner mindset rather than a job-worker mindset.

As homemakers, the home is ours to manage—to maximize, expand, and figure out. It takes strategy and insight. It takes long hours and interest. It takes dedication and a long view. The home is a business, not a job.

Homemakers, like business owners, have to be self-motivated and determine their own meaningful metrics without relying on others. Ownership means choosing and finding your own measurements and keeping yourself on target because you deeply care about moving your mission forward.

What more valuable product is there to put out into the world than a family? That's our mission.

Owners often delegate work to others but still take responsibility for the outcomes. They're interested not in getting a paycheck and clocking out for the weekend, but in putting something valuable out into the world. What more valuable product is there to put out into the world than a family? That's our mission.

Learn to Love What Must Be Done

I didn't want to hate housework anymore, but changing my attitude was not like a switch I could flip after so many years of inner grumbling. It was a long-haul, multi-year process to reorient my heart, mind, and actions to truth. It seemed so simple, but it was difficult. I was often discouraged because I thought I had flipped a switch, turned a corner, jumped on a new bandwagon and could now go my merry way, experiencing success after success. It didn't work that way.

If you search the internet for how to get started on a homemaking routine, most articles will say you should start getting organized by making your bed, which I had never done on principle. Such a waste of time. I was ready to change, though, and at least making a bed is quick and easy, so I followed common wisdom.

I couldn't understand it, though. Every time I tried to build the habit of making my bed and keeping my bedroom tidy, I felt uncomfortable. Internal resistance welled up, and I'd fall back into my old patterns of disheveled living before tidiness had a chance to take root.

Then, one day, I noticed something unusual. If I wasn't actively patting myself on the back for following through, I'd be internally grumping about said new habits, even while doing them. So instead of thinking about myself, whether feeling proud or disgruntled, I turned my attention to the work and environment outside myself. After making my bed, I'd pause and say, "Wow, that looks nice!" After hanging up my clothes or wiping down a counter, I'd pause and say to myself, "Oh, that *is* better."

Instead of noticing myself, I was *noticing the world around me*. Instead of thinking about how that world was affecting me, I was noticing how I was affecting the world. In this way, I stopped smack-talking repetitious work. Instead of calling mundane tasks pointless, I called them stewardship, ways to bless others.

Then, a funny thing happened. I realized one day that it didn't bother me to make the bed every single day. It was just what I did. It was more than a rote habit. I had practiced *rejoicing* in the repetition, not merely bearing it, and now the rejoicing was normal, not awkwardly forced. What at first had

Instead of noticing myself, I was *noticing the world around me*. Instead of thinking about how that world was affecting me, I was noticing how I was affecting the world.

felt impossible and uncomfortable became my new norm after a few years—yes, *years*—of deliberately remodeling my thought patterns.

Take a Baby Step to Love Being a Homemaker

As you build new and better habits, notice when you slip into grumbling, dismissing, and self-sympathy; replace those thoughts with three seconds of appreciating the good effect you have had on your environment.

> *Older women likewise are to be reverent in behavior, not slanderers or slaves to much wine. They are to teach what is good, and so train the young women to love their husbands and children, to be self-controlled, pure, working at home, kind, and submissive to their own husbands, that the word of God may not be reviled.*
>
> —Titus 2:3–5

4

What Is Organization?

Organization is being prepared to graciously handle life as it happens

They constantly try to escape
From the darkness outside and within
By dreaming of systems so perfect
that no one will need to be good.
But the man that is will shadow
The man that pretends to be.

—T. S. Eliot, "The Rock"

When I was a kid, I always procrastinated cleaning my room. My room was in the basement, so most of the time I could avoid scrutiny by keeping my door closed. Inevitably, though, there'd come a time when mom would directly tell me to clean my room. Resigned to my fate, I'd enter my room, close the door, turn on my music, and begin diligently rearranging my bookshelves.

After spending an hour or so beautifying my shelves, I'd think it was time to move on to some other project, so I'd shove my clothes under the bed, push everything on the top of my dresser down into a drawer, take out the garbage, make my bed, and call it clean.

I entered married life with this approach to home management. When the kitchen was a disaster zone, I started by alphabetizing my spices or making new labels for the fridge shelves. I claimed this impulse was a desire to organize. I do like to put things in order.

However, lurking behind my impulse was mere procrastination—procrastination with a thin veneer of productivity. "Quick, look busy!" my instincts cried, while also demanding I skimp on effort. True cleaning would take more energy. Making decisions about clutter would be taxing. Alphabetizing was easy.

When the end of the day came, I would feel like I had been busy but hadn't gotten anywhere. I would stew in discouragement because productive procrastination is more procrastination than productivity. It isn't satisfying.

Not all efforts at restoring order are created equal. Some are more meaningful and useful than others. We *can* over-organize. We can waste time organizing when we should be cleaning or having a heart-to-heart conversation with our teen. It's not uncommon for organizing to become a mask, a veneer of virtue to plaster over an avoidance of our primary duties.

> It's not uncommon for organizing to become a mask, a veneer of virtue to plaster over an avoidance of our primary duties.

Now, when I clean my room, I start by throwing away as much garbage as possible and emptying the wastebasket. I fold or hang up clothes that are out of place. I wipe down surfaces. Alphabetizing books, ordering shirts by sleeve length and color, and rearranging my bedside table are now reward tasks I can do after twenty minutes of actual work.

First, We Buy All the Cute Containers

Sometimes we think organization will solve our issues with homemaking. We think if we just get the right system in place, then we won't struggle so much. As we've already seen, this is the temptation of perfectionism. The truth is that putting stuff in logical places will not resolve relationship difficulties. Methodical, thorough lists will not increase our stamina or change our desires. Matching containers with cute labels will not change our habits.

When we wonder how to organize our life, we tend to imagine homes that magically stay clean without much effort. We picture shelves, closets, and counters where everything stays where it belongs, as if none of it is ever used.

Of course, in our homes, things are used—and usually not put back in the right place right away. The more people in a home, the more likely it is that things are not returned immediately to their proper places. The increased activity level comes with an increased amount of entropy, the natural pull toward disorder.

> The ideal home is a place of living, loving people, not of static scenes.

The right response is *not* to clamp down on the activity level. The solution isn't fewer people at home less, although that would help the house stay cleaner. The ideal home is a place of living, loving people, not of static scenes. Often, we attempt to control the chaos from the wrong end, cutting down the amount of life lived rather than increasing the amount of maintenance applied.

When we are truly organized, we are willing to continue making the effort of homemaking, to maintain the work consistently. It's less about the house being organized and more about organizing our own habits and expectations.

An organized family home and life does not look like a Pinterest board or Martha Stewart magazine spread. It looks like being prepared for life, and 80 percent of preparedness is mental. Organization starts with our attitude, with our mindset. If we want to know how to organize our lives, we need to begin by realizing that our attitude is under our control.

The problem is that we've allowed the media to define organization for us. They tell us that organization means having your act together. It means a place for everything and everything in its place—*all the time.* All you need is this container, that label, or this article's hack to attain this blessed state—and their idea of a blessed state is a house that looks like people don't live in it.

The actual dictionary definition of the verb "to organize," however, shows a broader understanding:

- to arrange into a structured whole; to order
- to make arrangements or preparations for; to coordinate

Being always ready is primarily an attitude, a mindset, a heart thing, and secondarily a state of preparedness in terms of the material resources we employ. Containers are not where organization begins. We coordinate ourselves, our stuff, our space, and our people in order to more effectively and more abundantly live out the mission God has given us.

The goal of organization and planning is not to be in control or look put-together. The goal is to be equipped and ready to respond obediently to God in the moment as He sends needs our way.

Organize with the End in Mind

We need to organize with the end—the primary purpose—in mind, and the end is this: We should pursue effective organization so that we can honor our commitments and responsibilities. We want to be people of integrity, and that means tracking our obligations and following through reliably on our duties. We also want to be good stewards of our time, stuff, and energy. Being organized is not a matter of appearance that can be documented by a photo, despite all the marketing out there that says otherwise. Being organized is another way of being responsible, of operating with integrity. If the cute labels on the matching containers are tangential to acting responsibly, they are also tangential to being organized.

The goal is to be equipped and ready to respond obediently to God in the moment as He sends needs our way.

We are given many gifts–abilities, energy, homes, family, community, opportunities–and we are called to make the best use of them all.

We are given many gifts—abilities, energy, homes, family, community, opportunities—and we are called to make the best use of them all. Organization is managing our resources to increase the good works we are available and able to accomplish.

When we are organized, we are more available to serve at a greater capacity. When we manage our resources and follow through on our commitments, we are more open and engaged, helping our family and others as needs arise. We're more confident and calmer in our choices, able to adapt as needed when we notice opportunities to serve.

If we approach organization from a desire to serve others better rather than to make ourselves more impressive, we will fall into discouragement less often because our heart is in the right place. Our attitude will be organized.

But What about All the Stuff?

Let's assume you've organized your attitude. Still, you look around your house, and you know there's more to getting organized than thinking better thoughts. Clutter, groceries, collections, supplies for hobbies, books, papers—our homes are stuffed to the gills with *stuff.* Should we just get rid of it all and make a fresh start?

It's tempting to want to go minimalist just to deal with the overflowing amount of stuff we have in our homes. But minimalism and chaos are not the only two options.

Instead of feeling like all the moving pieces, all the stuff, is a problem, a set of difficulties to overcome, we can see it as the game we're playing. Keeping the plates spinning, tracking inventory, directing a team of people (and machines)—this is our calling, and we can increase our skill and capacity for it through cheerful practice, as I said earlier.

In our homes, we manage both stuff and space, and the two often seem at war. Clutter decommissions our space, taking it out of action while not delivering any benefits. Clutter isn't just "stuff I don't like" (i.e., other people's stuff). It's stuff that doesn't have a home or that isn't in its home. One way we home-make is to make a home for all the things.

A home is a deliberately chosen space that something occupies. When it's in that space, it is "put away." When it is not in that space, it is clutter. Decluttering, tidying, and organizing are always a dance between stuff and space. If there's no space, then stuff has to go. If there's stuff, it will occupy space, so it must be intentionally given space to occupy. If you aren't going to give your stuff a place to belong, you need to get rid of it. There's no other option.

Perhaps the right home for an item is in the garbage or at Goodwill, but it gets tricky when we have to find a place for all the things that *do* need to stay in our homes. We free up our space so it can be used well. Giving our things appropriate homes, then putting those things in their homes is the process of decluttering and organizing stuff so we can manage space.

In a way, tidying up is a kind of decluttering. That's why decluttering never really ends. Our stuff will be used, and then it will need to be put away. New items will come into the house; some items will need to leave the house. Decluttering is part of the ebb and flow of life, not a project to check off.

It's easy to get distracted by organization projects like labeling shelves and getting rid of things, as if the goal is simply to have a photo-worthy setup or less stuff. But labels and Goodwill runs are simply potential steps toward the real goal of having a home for everything. Because our home has limited space, we need to keep our stuff within our limits—this is decluttering, and it's constant.

When we step back and see our work as making our home a place where people are grown and nurtured, our view of the stuff can snap into proper focus. I shouldn't be getting rid of my people's craft supplies because they're getting in my way or ruining my aesthetic. Instead, I should be helping my people keep track of their craft supplies by offering homes for those craft supplies—containers, shelves, cabinets—and prompts to put them away.

We don't want our attempts at organization to turn us into harpies. We want to bless our family with our efforts. As our children develop a variety of interests, they will need accessories, space, and mess. Our job isn't to minimize these

As our children develop a variety of interests, they will need accessories, space, and mess.

things, just to manage them as best we can because it's all evidence of a good life being enthusiastically lived.

The Only Kind of Control We Have Is Self-Control

Sometimes we conclude that because we can never reach and/or maintain our ideal level or style of organization, having an ideal at all is our problem. We're tempted to stop trying to clean the house, organize the toys, lose the weight, balance the budget, or train the children because we never reach our desired goal, or, if we do, it doesn't last long.

However, the real problem lies in thinking there's a finish line we're supposed to reach. Somehow, we have to forge a path between happy-go-lucky drifting and stressed-out rigidity. We can only do this if we embrace the way God made the world. God made the world for a purpose. He made *us* for a purpose. God's purpose for us is to glorify Him and enjoy Him forever. We begin that forever call here and now, in this life, in the midst of our day-to-day work.

If we live as though we have no purpose, no point we should be working toward, we are not walking in the truth. God is the One Who not only created our purpose—which means it's not ours to make up—He is also the One Who holds the future in His hands; we do not. He didn't give us an outward, visible finish line to attain in this life. He is always calling us ever onward and upward.

God keeps us on our toes. He works in us most during those times when the rug seems to have been pulled out from under us. His purposes are far beyond our scope, especially if our scope is decorating a mantel and keeping the counters spotless. He wants us to practice the fruits of the Spirit—and homemaking is just one avenue for that practice.

We might imagine that being organized means having life go our way. When we're organized, we think we'll be in control, so it will be OK. Not so. No matter how much we get organized, life will always be outside our control. But our response to life—our attitude—*is* fully within our control.

Being organized boils down to exercising self-control, not situation control. We control our follow-through, our actions, our responses to messes. Self-control is responsibility. Attached to it are all the other fruits of the Spirit God is working in us, including joy. Happiness doesn't come when we have everything lined up just so. It comes when we are walking in cheerful reliance on God to complete the good works He has begun in us.

What It Looks Like to Be Organized

Yes, I would call myself organized now, but I always hesitate to tell people I have a podcast, a course—and now a book—called *Simplified Organization*. The immediate assumption tends to be that I must have my whole life aesthetically put together, but that is far from the reality. I'm not overbearing or particular about where people put their stuff because that has nothing to do with organization.

Being organized boils down to exercising self-control, not situation control.

I call myself organized because I take daily, intentional steps to be prepared for noticing and following through on the good works God has prepared for me. I don't always know what they are ahead of time, but I'm willing and able to set aside my plans for the day when God takes things in a different direction. Organization begins with spending time daily in Scripture and prayer, because it's only through these means that we are able to notice what God has for us each day.

Organization begins with spending time daily in Scripture and prayer, because it's only through these means that we are able to notice what God has for us each day.

A few months ago, my adult son texted me with a request. He had just met with a real-estate client family who was moving to town, and they had no plans for dinner. It turned out, my son discovered, that we shared a mutual friend with this family. "Can you have them over for dinner? I know they'd appreciate it," he said. It was 3 p.m.

Dinner was already in the Instant Pot. There was enough, but it wasn't anything special. *Here I am, Lord.* Homemaking and hospitality mean offering what you have, welcoming people into your real life, not putting on a show to impress anyone. I thanked God for providing an opportunity on a day when I already had food ready. I thanked Him for prompting me to start dinner early. I hadn't known it when I started dinner, but clearly, this was His plan all along. After checking with my husband, I texted my son back with a hearty, "Sure! How about six o'clock?"

During our family prayers, my husband likes to pray that we will see needs and meet them. When we are organized, we are able to do that more and more. Organization isn't only about having dinner ready for unexpected company; it's also about being open-handed and unperturbed when your day takes a different turn than you expect.

When we are walking in the Spirit, pursuing the good works God is laying out before us, organization has nothing to do with appearing successful or impressive. It is a delight to live with your radar tuned and your hands ready for the opportunities God sends. It is a joy to be organized.

Take a Baby Step to Be More Organized

Pick one small surface and remove the things that don't belong there. If you can, put them away quickly; otherwise, just put them in a temporary holding place. Wipe the surface and arrange the remaining items neatly. Take a moment to appreciate the order you've created.

> *Therefore, my beloved brothers, be steadfast, immovable, always abounding in the work of the Lord, knowing that in the Lord your labor is not in vain.*
>
> —1 Corinthians 15:58

5

What Is Simplicity?

Keeping things simple means keeping things purposeful

> Holistic living means that your spiritual, relational, emotional, intellectual, physical, and financial lives are working together.
>
> —Tsh Oxenreider, *Organized Simplicity*

One evening, when I was four months postpartum, I was folding laundry. Everywhere my eyes landed, I saw work I ought to do. Nothing was satisfactory. I felt like I had been busy all day but getting nowhere. I indulged this story, replaying it over and over with each towel I folded, a towel I'd probably be washing again tomorrow. I sighed and said to my husband, "I am so behind. I am doing a terrible job. Everything is a disaster."

He looked at me quizzically. "What do you mean?" he asked. "You're doing fine! Everything seems mostly like normal to me." Instead of taking this as the encouragement it was intended to be, I twisted it in my mind, making up a new narrative: *This disastrous state is just normal at our house. I was fooling myself that I'd ever made any progress. The house was always this bad, and my husband was just used to it. He didn't expect me to do any better than this.*

Some days later, I was texting with a friend who lived out of state. I told her how discouraged I felt about the housework that never went away. I said, "I don't have baby blues or anything, but . . ." I don't remember what followed my "but," because she said, "How do you know you don't have baby blues?"

I wasn't the kind who would, that's how. Of course, for the last seven months, my baby never slept more than two hours together. Baby blues, sleep deprivation, whatever you wanted to call it—maybe my mental and emotional state wasn't rational, after all.

A few weeks later, I was conversing with an internet friend about the same struggles. She said I should focus on "building a livable life"—a life I enjoyed living. She did not at all mean that I should only do what I loved, but rather that it was possible to love my real life. A livable life is one wherein I stop focusing on reaching a final destination, give up indulging in false narratives that keep me stuck, and brush away the cobwebs of unreasonable expectations.

A livable life is one wherein I stop focusing on reaching a final destination, give up indulging in false narratives that keep me stuck, and brush away the cobwebs of unreasonable expectations.

At that time, a livable life meant getting outside for exercise, starting with the daily basics instead of deep-cleaning projects, and prioritizing sleep so I could be an attentive mother. Every season of life requires adjustment and reevaluation of the steps necessary for a livable family life.

We Can't Blame the Stuff

When we think of simple living, we tend to conjure up visions of bright white kitchens, uncluttered living rooms, and slow days. To achieve simplicity, we think we have to remove or replace everything until our life and home look good enough to go viral on Instagram. But this, friends, is not real-world simple living.

Simple living means you have direction, that all aspects of your life cohere around a single-minded focus. Everything you do moves your primary mission forward. Simplicity means your life is not compartmentalized. It means your energies are not scattershot across a wide field, aiming at no particular target.

Simplicity means your life is not compartmentalized.

Simplicity and minimalism are not synonyms, though they are often used that way. To be a minimalist, you do without as much as possible. Your goal is to see how far you can cut back. To simplify, however, is to make your life an integrated whole where nothing interferes with the integrity of that whole. To simplify is to ensure that the different elements of our schedule, of our work, of our interactions, harmonize and build one another up.

> Simplified organization is organization that addresses the true disorder in our life.

Simplified organization is organization that addresses the true disorder in our life, not only the surface-level disorder of our counters or closets or cupboards, but the disorder in our mind and our heart. Until inner order prevails, outer order will be ineffectual, if it's even possible. It is only when we cut through the superficial answers and the impressive-looking solutions that we can understand what we want when we say we want to be organized or live more simply.

When we clean and contain our clutter in hopes that it will change our character, we're bound not only to be disappointed, we're also bound to return to our messy ways. The clutter will return. The disorder will continue. Its true source is not our circumstances but ourselves.

In my boom-and-bust pattern, I would go all-out and clean the whole house from top to bottom in a mad frenzy. I would bask in the glow of completion, then collapse. I repeated the process when the chaos was too terrible to put up with anymore. It was not integrity. It was not simple living.

The solution was not to clear all the stuff out of my house so I wouldn't have to clean anything anymore, as tempting as that option was. The real solution was to change my attitude, to see the significance of the work, to apply myself with faithfulness to my duties. I had to take joy in my own livable life, not wait for joy until my life looked the way I wanted it to.

Outer Order Begins with Inner Order

A friend of mine likes to divide people into two groups: maximizers and simplifiers. Maximizers love to see potential. They strategize about how to turn potential into actual. Simplifiers, on the other hand, see everything nonessential to a goal as clutter to be cleared away so the goal is clear and attainable.

Someone might look at my calendar these days—with two teens and a ten-year-old still at home—and assume I'm a maximizer. In fact, my current calendar probably would have sent the me of ten years ago into a panic. However, my friends would rightly tell you I'm a confirmed simplifier.

For example, the work I do writing, podcasting, and running an online business reinforces and improves the work I do around the house. I am better engaged with my real-life homemaking by writing about the purpose and importance of homemaking. It looks like I'm doing lots of things, but in my mind, I'm focusing on one thing.

I learn my own lessons more deeply by sharing them with others. I practice skills of organization and management in a different area—running a business and managing a team—that translate into improved skills in managing a household. When I level up in one area of life, I'm leveling up my competency and capacity across all areas, because I'm bringing the same self to each one.

To be organized is to live in an orderly fashion, not only with your stuff, but in your mind. Organizing your stuff will not bring you into a state of inner harmony and peace, though that is what magazines promise. We believe the marketer's promise and repeat it to ourselves. If only we could declutter and organize, then we'd be happy.

After all, our search for organization is a search for happiness, for integration, for wholeness. We are spiritual beings as well as material beings, and if we function as if we and the world are merely physical, we will never achieve the inner harmony, the inner order we are looking for. We should integrate our actions, ideals, and feelings because God made us and the world to operate in an integrated way.

That's why, if we do find inner order, it will work itself into outer order. Once our mindset, our attitude, and our approach become organized, then we become able to work out a physical, material organization that sticks. It sticks because we know it's not what matters most, because we know that sticking doesn't mean permanence, but rather an approach worked out and worked on continually.

This might sound more like complicated organization than simplified organization, but it isn't. We grumble about our work because our desire is to get to the point where we won't have to work anymore. However, that's not the way God made the world. We will always have work to do. When we address our root attitude issues, we begin to experience the kind of progress we never saw when we tried for surface-level organization.

Simplify by Knowing What You're About

When we simplify organization, we cut to the heart first and realize that stuff-management is a way we extend a blessing to others (and ourselves). It is not a thing that bestows blessing by itself; it is not pixie dust that makes everything better. It is a tool, a way of life that is consistent with our character once we have aligned our thoughts and feelings with truth.

We can weave our various responsibilities into a unified whole when we think of homemaking as our primary vocation. The word "vocation" comes from the Latin *vocare*, which means "to call." Often, vocation is used as a synonym for one's career, but within Christian thought over the centuries, it has also connotated duties that God has given.

The key to the Christian concept of vocation, or calling, is that it comes from outside of us. We don't call ourselves; therefore, we are not accountable to ourselves alone. God calls us, so we are accountable to God. Yes, this ups the stakes, but it's only when we rightly relate to our Lord that we can enjoy the life He has called us to.

As a vocation, the work of homemaking is a responsibility, a duty, which means it determines what ends up on our calendar, what ends up on the to-do list, and what ends up claiming our attention and energy each day. To call homemaking a vocation is to remember that we do not determine our own mission or our own destiny. Open-handed trust on the one hand and purposeful direction on the other are harmonized in the concept of vocation.

It's easy to fixate on who we wish we were or who we want to become. Such thoughts usually lead us to despair because we never live up to our own standard. However, seeing homemaking as our vocation reminds us that we're not working on a task to check off. We're living within a capacity, working out a calling. Our vocation is a compass, directing our movement forward.

> To call homemaking a vocation is to remember that we do not determine our own mission or our own destiny.

The truth is, we don't know what will happen today, much less what will happen in a year, five years, or a lifetime. We don't know how long our lifetime will be. What we do know is that we are where God has placed us, that God has given us duties to perform here and now, and that He is using those duties to further equip us for duties He will give us in the future.

Because He has called us, given us a vocation in which to serve Him, we can know whether or not we are on the right track. We simply ask, are we accepting our work with joy and gratitude, or moping and complaining about it?

Simple Doesn't Mean Easy or Effortless

In an age of instant gratification, we easily fall into a bad attitude about work. We seek out routines, habits, and plans that promise to reduce the time and effort involved in our work. Although routines and habits do make things easier, they do so by reducing the mental effort of decision-making and by increasing our strength and stamina through practice. The work itself will always take time and energy—and that's OK.

I spent far too many years looking for ways to put in minimal effort around the house. Minimal effort gets minimal results, no matter how you cut it. Minimal effort puts you on the fast track to chaos and lethargy. When I was in my twenties, I thought that if I put minimal energy into chores, I'd have tons of energy left for the projects I *wanted* to work on. I was wrong.

I found that choosing minimal energy in my responsibilities led to putting forth minimal effort anywhere unless I got that deadline-panic rush. Once I began to be convicted that my home was worth my time and energy and started applying myself, I found I had more to go around, not less. My worries about burnout were unfounded. More of God's will in my life was better, not worse.

Some say it is the decrease in environmental chaos that increases our energy. While I do think that's part of it, I also think there are some Newtonian physics at play—that is, God made the world to work this way. Objects at rest tend to stay at rest, and objects in motion tend to stay in motion. When we get going around the house, we find satisfaction and natural momentum. Our energy builds when we begin with our responsibilities.

We get the process entirely backward when we search for the perfect, elaborate plan that will finally allow us to keep a clean and tidy house with minimal effort. Instead, when we start with effort invested in the basic, core processes of our home—kitchen, laundry, bathrooms, and tidying—we find that our interest and motivation in those areas improves naturally.

If we wait for inspiration to get started, we won't begin until the deadline-induced panic hits. That's not the kind of inspiration we want to be operating from. Inspiration—and even affection, a change of orientation and attitude—will follow simple steps of faithfulness and lead to lasting change. The simple steps matter most. The simple steps will lead us onward and upward.

Start Simply and Simply Start

The simple steps matter most. The simple steps will lead us onward and upward.

I tend to squeeze a lot out of my days at this point in my life, in my forties with teenagers and a busy life. However, I have not graduated beyond needing to start simply—and simply start. In fact, it's because I've embraced starting simply that I am able to juggle more than I used to.

In my thirties, I would make an elaborate plan for using up all of my day completely efficiently. I would then proceed to totally ignore that plan, even spending chunks of time zoned out on the couch as if I had no plan or direction at all. My problem was twofold.

First, I was ignoring the nature of my responsibilities at the time. I had a house full of children, from teens to preschoolers, home all day every day, needing mothering at unpredictable moments and in unpredictable ways. Scheduling my day as if I was the master of my time did not match my reality. Mothering isn't the kind of responsibility that can be penciled into a time slot on your calendar.

Second, deep down, I knew my plan was unrealistic, that I would not keep it up, and so my perfectionism would flare up, and I would not even start something that wasn't going to work. I discounted the effect I could have in any one area in a mere five or ten minutes. I thought I needed thirty or forty or ninety minutes to do anything significant, and I never knew if I'd really have that much time uninterrupted (probably not). Waiting for the perfect moment, I frittered away my time in distraction.

My children need me less now, so I have more uninterrupted time, but this is not the biggest change. The most significant change, the change that kicked me out of despair mode, out of woe-is-me mode when my day didn't go as planned, was recognizing that *five minutes makes a difference.*

I don't have to be certain that I'm doing the very most important thing at any given moment; I just need to do something I *ought* to be doing. I don't wait until I know I have a full hour, I just tell myself, "Start with five minutes and see what happens." Getting up and getting moving builds momentum and clarity, while sitting and mulling never does. If I wash a few of the dishes, it's better than washing none of the dishes, even if I don't get to them all.

If I start, I might actually finish, but there's no way the dishes will get done if I never start. I might not have a full plan for dinner, but I can pull out some meat and start tidying the kitchen, and inspiration is more likely to hit than if I wait for it on the couch. Five minutes makes a difference, not only in getting something done, but also in changing the direction and intensity of your energy. Energy increases with movement.

> I don't have to be certain that I'm doing the very most important thing at any given moment; I just need to do something I *ought* to be doing.

Take a Baby Step to Simplify Your Homemaking

Take a picture of your kitchen. Spend five minutes—use a timer—tidying things up and cleaning. Take another picture after the five minutes are up. Notice the difference you were able to make in such a short time.

> *The wisest of women builds her house, but folly with her own hands tears it down.*
>
> —Proverbs 14:1

6

What Is Productivity?

Productivity is not efficiency but faithful fruitfulness

As Christians, we are called to do hard work, but never by ourselves. God promises to help every Christian who is engaged in the pursuit of godliness. He is not going to do it for us, but He promises to do it with us. That is why we do not surrender to despair when we fail—and we frequently do fail—in our pursuit of sanctification. God will give us the grace, and He promises His help.

—R. C. Sproul, *Truths We Confess: A Systematic Exposition of the Westminster Confession of Faith*

I first read David Allen's *Getting Things Done* while nursing my third child. Twenty-five years old, I highlighted, took notes, and was pretty sure I had discovered the solution to all my home management woes. I brain dumped. I made all the lists he specified. I started trying to practice a "Weekly Review" of my home the way

Allen instructed executives to wrap up every loose end every Friday.

My initial excitement fell back into apathetic discouragement. A few months later, nursing, staring out the window, I tried imagining ways to make my life work more like an office worker's job. I dreamed about what I could do if I was able to metaphorically "close my office door" and focus on whatever I was doing without the interruptions of little people.

At the time, the life of a CEO with an assistant and a workday that did not include stepping on Cheerios or LEGOs seemed wonderful. Theoretically and abstractly, I knew my work as a mom was more fundamental and more meaningful, but practically, it sure didn't feel like it. My work was the thankless work that people only notice when it's not done, rather than when it's done well.

The office life lends itself to a more compartmentalized way of living. You arrive at the office, you do the things, you clock out and go home. Motherhood and homemaking are not like that. Instead, we're "on call" all day and all night. Everything we do affects other people directly—and what other people do directly affects our workload and our emotional load.

If we believe an office-based life is the standard, then the always-on nature of homemaking will feel chaotic, demeaning, and pointless. But why do such a thing? Office-based jobs are a fairly recent phenomenon if we look back across time and cultures—but motherhood and homemaking go all the way back historically and all the way across culturally. Which scenario provides a more human outlook on life? Which is more in tune with how we were designed?

After realizing that the business-book approach was becoming a snare to my attitude, I went on my Austen and Dickens novel-reading kick. Both authors understood human nature, community needs, and moral standards. Both depict true-to-life female archetypes that can open our eyes not only to our own particular foibles, but also to our particular function in society. Stories provided a better grounding for approaching my life than "practical" productivity books, whether business- or home-centric.

We Need More Than Grades and Gold Stars

When we focus on the wrong kind of productivity, we see our work as a mere set of tasks to be checked off, more or less efficiently. But homemaking is not a janitorial job, where you perform the checklist and then move on to the rest of your life with plenty of free time. In reality, homemaking is an entrepreneurial pursuit. Each woman runs her own unique little business, with innumerable pieces contributing to the overall effect and bottom-line result.

When we come to housework, cooking, and even parenting with a "clock in and do the checklist" mentality, we end the day overloaded and undone. There are so many plates we're supposed to keep spinning that we can't even track them all down—especially when several have rolled down the hall and around the corner.

The job-worker mentality has no place for mothers at home. Our home business is the business of caretaking. Caretaking requires attentiveness of a different nature than any other industry, but it's work women were designed to excel in. Caretaking—homemaking—precedes any other economic endeavor; without secure and steady homes, societies and economies crumble.

We've all seen those online articles, calculating what a mother would earn on the free market. No matter how high a wage it estimates for motherhood and homemaking, we all know it's ridiculous. There is no price we can put on late-night feedings, on intense parenting conversations, on making a grocery trip both frugal money management and fun field trip. Some people might have nannies and personal chefs to whom they pay a salary, but such jobs don't set the standard by which a mother's value is determined.

Sure, most business owners get a paycheck—from themselves, not from an employer—but they run their business for more than the paycheck. They enjoy the challenge of creatively and compellingly filling needs. As homemakers, we need to own the home as a creative endeavor we can maximize, expand, and figure out. It takes strategy and insight. It takes focus, dedication, and long hours. It takes the long view. The home is a business that is prerequisite to all other businesses, because the home's business is people.

Homemakers, like business owners, have to be self-motivated and determine their own meaningful metrics without relying on feedback from others. Ownership means choosing and finding your own measurements and keeping yourself on target because you care deeply about moving your mission forward.

Homemaking is not about financial profit, but it *is* a way of turning profit on the talents, resources, and situation God has given us. He gives us gifts not so we can spend the majority of our time sitting back and enjoying them in ease and comfort, but so that we can invest them, increasing them through wise management. The fastest way to multiply what God has given us is by investing in other people. And the primary means of investing in people is the family.

> Homemaking is not about financial profit, but it *is* a way of turning profit on the talents, resources, and situation God has given us.

The Productive Christian Household

If you browse social media or even the latest books on organizing or homemaking, the primary image of the home is a place of retreat and refuge. The world is where the action is, where the paycheck comes from, and where we go out and get dirty. The home, in this view, is where we return to get cleaned up and rest. However, this view of the household is a post-industrial ideal.

The home, biblically and historically, is not primarily a place for hygge, for coziness, for retreat. The home is where the primary action of culture happens; so much action happens here that it spills out into the wider world. A man and a woman come together to form a new household, and their union produces children, the most valuable asset of any society.

Children are not the accessories of a picture-perfect lifestyle, given to us so we can take cute photos. Children are future men and women. Children are our connection to and investment in the future. Without children, a society has no future. Therefore, raising children is one of the most productive things we can do. It's also one of the least efficient things we can do—and therein lies the struggle.

> Children are our connection to and investment in the future.

The world's version of productivity looks like putting in the minimum amount of effort possible while still getting a worthwhile return. Productivity tips and tricks generally revolve around minimizing effort while still getting results. That might be a great model for factories, but factories are bad analogies for people and life. The principles don't cross over.

When we look at biblical analogies for effort and productivity, we see not only imagery of fruitfulness, but also of athletics. Here is one arena the world still understands and honors. Top athletes are obsessive. Every day doesn't win them a gold medal—the gold medal lies at the end of the race. Before the race comes grueling, repetitive training that the athlete invests in because of the medal set before him. He disciplines his body. Everything he eats, does, and thinks supports his mission.

The apostle Paul speaks this way of the Christian life: "Do you not know that in a race all the runners run, but only one receives the prize? So run that you may obtain it" (1 Cor. 9:24). We're not called to be slacker Christians, putting in just enough effort to get us to the finish line someday. We are called to be a visible, bright, shining light on a hill that non-Christians can't help but notice and credit to God (Matt. 5:16).

God saves us by Christ alone. Only Christ's work imputed to us makes us right with God. Yet after we are saved, after God has renewed our heart, He calls us to strenuous effort for Him; He makes us His slaves for righteousness now that we are no longer slaves to sin (Rom. 6:19). As Philippians 2:12–13 tells us, "Work out your own salvation with fear and trembling, for it is God who works in you, both to will and to work for his good pleasure."

Productivity, work, and effort are not optional for Christians, but rather commanded. A productive Christian household is a household on mission for the kingdom, an outpost of the gospel, even in details like cleaning the bathroom and doing the laundry. God created the family to be the base unit of society, not just for the propagation of the human race but for the sanctification of every member.

It is primarily through our familial bonds that we are transformed and sanctified.

It is primarily through our familial bonds that we are transformed and sanctified. As Hermann Bavinck writes in *The Christian Family*, "The family is the school of life, because it is the fountain and hearth of life." He goes on to say, "The family transforms ambition into service, miserliness into munificence, the weak into strong, cowards into heroes, coarse fathers into mild lambs, tenderhearted mothers into ferocious lionesses. Imagine there were no marriage and family; humanity would, to use Calvin's crass expression, turn into a pigsty."

Our productivity and dedication—our diligence—intensifies when we realize that we are not mere cooks and janitors cleaning up after people because somebody had to be stuck with that job. When we understand that our role within our families is raising immortal souls to glorify their Creator forever, weaving the fabric of society and becoming more like our Savior as we do, it makes sense that we're called to work hard.

Productivity as Faithful Fruitfulness

Although we think we want to *be* productive, what we actually want is to *feel* productive. Being productive while feeling crummy stinks. I don't want an empty feel-good vibe, but neglecting the feel-good doesn't work, either. Trust me, I've tried. When productivity feels good, it feels energizing. That energy, in turn, helps us keep going. When productivity feels bad, it feels like walking dead, like the slow sapping of vitality with each checked-off task on the stupid list.

The difference between productivity feeling bad or good is not the work being done but our feelings about the work. This is why our attitudes are so important to our organization. We have things we need to get done every day. We have people we need to build up. We have homes to manage. We have good works God has called us to. It is possible to take joy in those good works—all of them—because of the One Who sends them.

A productive day is one wherein we respond in trust, with steadfastness and faithfulness, to the circumstances God sends us. That is how He produces in us the fruit of His Spirit, which is the productivity He desires. Our productivity, our fruitfulness in our homes, is not about measurable successes. We can find joy and satisfaction in each cup of cold water given, each face washed and kissed, each meal set on the table, each sweeping of the floor, because these are our deposits in the investment of building God's kingdom through the care of His people.

When we are in the thick of the season where our primary good works revolve around raising children, it can feel like everything we do is too little and too mundane to be significant. Yet remember that Christ said, "As you did it to one of the least of these my brothers, you did it to me." Our own children are not excluded from this. It's easy to feel like they are getting in the way of what we are trying to do, but they *are* what we are trying to do.

We have to watch our story, our metaphor, of productivity. Productivity and organization techniques aren't upgrades to

> We are like trees in God's orchard. All our lives, we are watered and pruned by God.

our engines or accelerators on the track of life. We aren't like machines; we are like trees in God's orchard. All our lives, we are watered and pruned by God.

We never get to a point when we no longer need to bring in new nutrients, to be watered by the Word and sacraments, to be pruned and shaped by trial and testing for the purpose of bringing more and better glory to God in our fruitful obedience. All our lives, we go through season after season of visibly ripening fruit and dormancy.

We need to be well-watered trees producing abundant crops in God's timing, not our own. He is the Lord of the harvest. We tend to think of productivity as the ability to be laser-focused with high-achievement outcomes. Fruitfulness shifts the imagery and, therefore, the expectation. A fruitful tree is messy. In every direction, branches reach outward. A fruitful tree is stationary yet exhibits growth and movement.

Typical modern productivity imagery feels more like a freight train, powering forward unilaterally; productivity is the speed at which the train is able to reach its destination. Fruit, on the other hand, is seasonal. Fruitfulness has no destination. It will stop only at death. Fruit trees require continual sunshine, pruning, fertilizer, water, and growth. It is the same with us.

When we adopt fruitfulness as our metaphor for productivity, it realigns not only our motivation, but also our attitudes. Not every piece of fruit on a tree has to be amazing for the tree to be productive and plentiful. Even some of the good fruit falls to the ground, yet this is one way God provides food for the birds and other creatures we never see.

When we are fruitful trees, we don't have to be the harvester and warehouser and chef, concerned about how the fruit is used after it is produced. We aren't more fruitful if more of our fruit is used to make pies than juice. God is the harvester, field manager, and chef. We can be joyfully abundant because the work comes from God, we get to direct it back to God, and He manages the results.

Feeling productive while being productive comes when we focus on our current season, on the needs in front of us, on the next small task rather than a grand scheme or a lifetime mission. Our productivity doesn't have to be measurable to be appreciated or significant. Fruitfulness is a metaphor we as women can particularly embrace and embody because fruit is female. Fruitfulness is our design feature.

Fruitfulness is a perfect metaphor for productivity because what God is working in us is a harvest of the fruits of the Spirit: love, joy, peace, patience, kindness, goodness, faithfulness, gentleness, and self-control. These fruits are never abstract or theoretical. Each smile at a child, each mess cleaned up, each squabble adjudicated counts as a fruitful step on our path of sanctification.

Productivity as a Secret Sauce

I'm always tempted to get obsessive about some new hobby or project that's caught my fancy. Productivity seems like the secret sauce that will help me maximize the time I can spend on my current whim. But in reality, faithful productivity keeps me on target, focused on what truly matters rather than what has currently captured my attention.

For example, when I sit with my coffee on a typical homeschool morning, I usually look around and see all manner of home projects I "need" to tackle. The baseboards are dusty, the pantry is a jumble, extra dishes wait on the counter to be washed, the oven smells like it needs a good cleaning—there is always maintenance and improvement work to be done in a home.

But the work of the morning is educating my children. The oven, the pantry, the dust can wait—and will likely wait for weeks. Spending my time noticing all those areas, allowing them to nag me and pull away my attention, is a distraction and a temptation. Productivity is not about getting everything done; it's about getting the *right* things done.

It can feel productive to notice something and immediately start working on it, but I've had to cultivate the self-discipline to stay on target rather than veer off wherever my attention happens to wander. There's no secret sauce that makes this easy. There's no special tactic that prevents my homemaker-radar from blinking red when I see spots on the floor or piles of coats tangled up in piles of shoes.

Just as I require my children to come and do their math no matter what grand moment of LEGO inspiration they are currently experiencing, just as my husband shows up at work no matter how he feels, so I also have to show up to the day's work. Satisfaction and joy come after we've surmounted the hump of getting started.

Inspiration and enthusiasm are good servants when they follow the train of diligence. However, if I let them drive the train, I can spend the whole day being busy at unimportant work while neglecting my family. Diligent, prudent, fruitful productivity simply shows up to do that day's work. The more I've practiced showing up and starting, whether I feel like it or not, the more often I *do* end up feeling like it.

Take a Baby Step to Increase Productivity

As the mother setting the tone of a home and building up a family, one of the most productive things you can do is smile more at your people. Your cheerful, loving demeanor builds people, builds cultures, and builds your own work ethic.

> *For the grace of God has appeared, bringing salvation for all people, training us to renounce ungodliness and worldly passions, and to live self-controlled, upright, and godly lives in the present age, waiting for our blessed hope, the appearing of the glory of our great God and Savior Jesus Christ, who gave himself for us to redeem us from all lawlessness and to purify for himself a people for his own possession who are zealous for good works.*
>
> —Titus 2:11–14

PART 2

Six Steps Toward Skillful Homemaking

Fill thou my life, O Lord my God,
in every part with praise,
That my whole being may proclaim
thy being and thy ways.
Not for the lip of praise alone,
nor e'en the praising heart,
I ask, but for a life
made up of praise in ev'ry part:

Praise in the common words I speak,
life's common looks and tones,
In fellowship enjoyed at home
with my beloved ones,
Enduring wrong, reproach, or loss
with sweet and steadfast will,
Forgiving freely those who hate,
returning good for ill.

So shall each fear, each fret, each care
be turned into a song,
And ev'ry winding of the way
the echo shall prolong.
So shall no part of day or night
from sacredness be free,
But all my life, in ev'ry step,
be fellowship with thee.

Horatius Bonar, 1866

7

Step 1: Tell True Stories

We can change how we feel about our lives by changing our inner narrator

Your life will contribute to a grand and wonderful story no matter what you do. You have been spoken. You are here, existing, choosing, living, shaping the future and carving the past . . . We will contribute to this narrative. But how?

—N. D. Wilson, *Death by Living: Life Is Meant to Be Spent*

When I was big-pregnant with my youngest, I had to turn slightly sideways to reach the kitchen faucet and turn on the water. With my arms all the way outstretched, I could manage to wash the pots and pans in the deep, apron-front sink, but just barely.

One evening, as I was washing dishes and everyone else was clearing the table, my husband watched me for a moment and then said, "Hey, I'm going to wash the dishes. You go sit and put your feet up." Swollen ankles and all, I'm sure I looked rather pitiful.

The next evening at dinner he said, "Doing the dinner dishes is my job now. You rest."

That baby was born via C-section, so my husband took over all the dishes and more while I recovered. When I was back on my feet, though, clearing the dinner table and starting the dishes, he said, "Hey, why are you taking my job?"

For years, he did the dinner dishes every night. I'd wipe down the counters and sweep while he washed, and we'd talk. Cleaning up the kitchen together in the evening was like a mini-date, the kind of mini-date you only appreciate after you've spent over a decade together. Yes, I appreciated his help with the dishes. However, more than helping with the chores, his perspective on doing the work itself was an encouragement.

He's a programmer, so his workday is spent sitting at a computer, manipulating symbols on a screen. Having grown up on an orchard, driving a tractor and harvesting fruit, the shift to sedentary and abstract work sometimes chafes him. Washing dishes, he told me, was a great way to end the day. In his work, he'd wonder if he really *did* anything. Dishes, on the other hand, were definitely done. With your hands in the water and suds, you transform something from dirty to clean, and it's inherently satisfying.

As he explained why he wanted to keep doing the dishes, my mind reeled. Here, my own bad attitude about dishes, laundry, and almost every other chore was confronted and upended.

I disliked housework because I resented that it would all have to be done again tomorrow. No matter how good or bad a job you do, it will need to be done again. Now, here was my husband, telling me he enjoyed doing the dishes because it was real, tangible work accomplished, but I had always thought of it as work that was never accomplished.

Looking at the same job, we told opposite stories about it.

Do You See What I See?

We've all experienced a situation wherein two people receive the same facts, yet walk away with totally different interpretations of those facts. The interpretation is our story, the way we make sense of the details and weave them together into a connected whole.

Even when our facts are straight, our stories can be completely backward. It's like we have a narrator, a sportscaster, always running in the background of our minds, fitting the details we see into a grid to make sense of it all. We often see the story we're imposing on our life through the metaphors we use to describe our life. Is life a rat race? A hamster wheel? A crazy bus?

What we compare ourselves, our people, and our lives to matters immensely. Humans reason by analogy. A is like B, so B tells me about how to handle A.

If our brains are like computers, and if our individuality resides in our brain, then we expect to run systems like software on autopilot, power on and off at will, and reason logically. If our life is like a rat race, then we expect it to be busy and unfulfilling except for the occasional bite of cheese we might find.

Those metaphors might seem like they fit, but in truth, I am making them fit by returning again and again to my chosen version of the story. The details of my life that support this story become the details I notice most. Without intending to, I've installed a filter that causes me to interpret life as frustrating, overwhelming, and impossible.

Often, the biggest roadblock to joy and satisfaction in our home life is our own perspective, our internal interpretive grid. Reframing the story we see ourselves playing out is how we begin to organize our attitude.

We might not even realize we're telling false stories. We usually think we're just telling it like it is. Like the time I said to my husband in the evening, "Ugh, I didn't get anything done today!" I knew what was on my to-do list and what a small fraction of it I'd completed. He didn't know my list, but he worked from home and had seen throughout the day what I'd been doing.

He looked at me, eyebrows raised, and said, "Stop lying to yourself." That stopped me in my tracks. So, instead of complaining, I told him the things that I *had* done, things that mattered even though they weren't the things that were on my list. I replaced my false story with a true story.

Much of our unhappiness and negativity arises from not taking our thoughts captive as Scripture commands. We allow any grumblings that enter our head to take up residence. We call these thoughts and feelings authentic and real because they happened to us. These default responses demand to be stars in our story, shaping our perception of reality.

However, just because a thought or feeling comes naturally does not automatically make it worth our attention or necessary to our story. We need to ask: *Are these thoughts true?* If we want truth to become increasingly authentic in our lives, then we have to take control of the thoughts we allow to have airtime within our head.

That which we repeat, we will become, so let's take charge and repeat truth to ourselves. Let's not entertain complaining, whining, discouraging, or lying thoughts. The more we remind ourselves of truth and place ourselves within the context of truth, the more we will see truth instead of lies in our life story.

God Is the Author of Your Story

Your life is the story of you. This means that right now, today, you are living your biography. What will be included in your biography? What types of events are included in the biographies of great people? What types of events are included in biographies that are fascinating to read? Every interesting story, whether fact or fiction, hinges on a problem or tension a character must face. The story revolves around the character's decisions at various testing points and the consequences downstream from those decisions.

Your responses determine what kind of character you are. If you imagine yourself as a kind, loving, diligent mother, then you have to be kind even when the children are not, loving even when the children are resistant, and diligent even when you're tired. Reading and thinking about virtues is not adequate; virtues are developed through practice.

The temptation to become irritable is precisely the story-moment wherein patience is developed. Patience is not developed when nothing occurs that irritates or frustrates us. Patience comes when we exercise it, and we can't exercise it without the difficulty that demands it. Instead of being caught up in the heat of the moment, look at points of temptation as your biography in progress. How would you want this scene to be written? What would you want said of you? Make that true by living it now.

Good stories have plots. They are never random, never governed by chance. We do live out a story, because God is sovereign, and He is weaving everything to fit His purposes. Not a single sparrow falls apart from God's will (Matt. 10:29). He knows every hair on our head. He has purchased our life for Himself and is preparing us to spend eternity with Him.

Life is not a random series of events. History is not random, either. Each story, no matter how big or small, is God's story of creation, fall, and redemption. We aren't riding the waves of chance. God as Creator means God as Author. He has told us how His stories go: He makes all things new. He is weaving the gospel right into our life story. We can have peace and joy because He is trustworthy and in control. As the children's Sunday school song reminds us, He has the whole world in His hands.

We have to be willing to call ourselves out when we catch ourselves grumbling about our life. All complaints are ultimately ingratitude to God, unbelief that He is doing good to and for us. But we shouldn't merely accuse ourselves; accusation alone would leave us stuck in a guilt cul-de-sac. We repent of all complaining and grumbling, which means turning away from it. We must replace any internal lies with truth. What is the truth of the situation? Repeat that intentionally.

We are characters in God's story of redemption—His redemption of us as individuals and His redemption of a people through all history. From the very first day of history to the very last, God is telling a story. Sometimes the plot points our Author has assigned us are not what we would have written for ourselves, but we can trust Him as the One Who knows the beginning from the end, Who holds the whole world in His hands, Who knows what we need more than we do. Therefore, we must not complain, but walk in faith.

After all, the Author has told us His overarching plot line and how it all works out in the end: creation, fall, redemption. So, as we narrate our story to ourselves—and to others—while living it out, we can always keep faithful to the revealed plot of Christ's grace given on the cross, grateful to our loving and sovereign Author.

What If You Are the Supporting Character and Not the Star?

While it's true that each of our own lives is a story, this means that other people are living their stories adjacent to our own. We are not only the protagonists of our own personal dramas. We are also supporting characters in other people's stories. What role are we playing in the stories of others?

As we handle our own conflict and development, we can better understand how to respond when we see the story with perspective. Perspective is viewing an object from a distance, from a different angle, to get a more complete understanding. In our interactions with others, we can consider a story from the perspective of the other person as the protagonist. Taking such a view is one way to "look not only to [our] own interests, but also to the interests of others" (Phil. 2:4).

When we outfit our children for the coming winter, when we greet our husband with a kiss, when we sit at the table and smile at our people, when we stock the cupboards, we are setting the stage and providing for the stories of others. We are being good supporting characters.

When I am upset with my children because they scrawled on the wall with marker, walked on the freshly mopped floor with dirty feet, or failed to keep their room tidy, the story I see is one where they are imps and villains ruining my carefully orchestrated set. I see only *my* story, and they are messing it up.

A truer perspective would see the child as the hero of his own story, placed in my home so I can be his guide and coach, preparing him for his coming of age. If I look at it that way, the walls, floor, and bedroom are not about me, so I have no reason to be offended. I am only seeing the next scene in my child's character development—and I get to help it happen.

What kind of a character am I in my children's lives? What kind of a character am I in my husband's narrative? What kind of a character am I in my church community? What is my character in the stories of other people's lives? The wicked stepmother? The nagging wife? The gossipy friend? The kind of character I am in other people's stories tells what kind of character I truly have.

The kind of character I am in other people's stories tells what kind of character I truly have.

Change the Story You're Telling

Thinking about life as a story helps keep the present—even present chaos—in perspective. It's a way to think about the present in light of the past and the future. It doesn't have to be complicated. If I am a character in a story, and if that story continues past this moment, then what I do now shapes what happens next in my story. It's pretty simple, yet pretty revolutionary.

We are always thinking about our life as a story, we're just usually not aware of it. Complaints are false stories we tell about our situation. In the Old Testament, when the Israelites focused on the hot sand, the wandering path, and the unknown future, they started telling themselves that slavery in Egypt was not so bad. They had a varied diet in Egypt, at least, and a clear purpose to accomplish each day.

An ungrateful, dissatisfied heart leads us to glaring misreadings of our story, just like the Israelites. To avoid this, we have to be intentional and proactive, rooting out complaints before they taint our perspective. However, you can't just remove complaints. You have to *replace* them.

We *will* tell a story about our life. Every complaint-based story must be replaced with a gratitude-based story. How does faith reinterpret this same situation? How does love spin this circumstance? Choose *that* story to tell. It will feel awkward and maybe even fake at first, but rejecting a grumbling attitude and replacing it with a grateful one is worth the discomfort.

Over time, a rejoicing heart becomes our norm as we practice gratitude and walk in Christ's forgiveness, extending it as we have received it. When we've become accustomed to rejoicing, our interpretive grid is tuned to truth, tuned to see God at work where once we saw only problems and trouble. We can submit to and even enjoy the story God is telling in our life if we are in prayer, in constant conversation with God throughout the day.

Where our thoughts dwell makes all the difference in how we interpret what's happening. The psalms speak constantly of meditation, and in the New Testament, we are exhorted to meditate on what is good and true and upright and beautiful. Biblical meditation is a filling of the mind, not an emptying. Meditation is how we keep a proper perspective and align our judgement with God's, so we are more and more likely to see our situation from God's perspective.

However, in order to meditate on the truth, we have to *know* truth. To know truth, we have to be filling our mind with truth. Daily Bible reading and prayer are essential to an aligned and vibrant attitude. Without it, we are tossed on the winds of our emotions. We need the centering and stabilizing of God's Word for our heart and mind.

> To know truth, we have to be filling our mind with truth.

We need to be in the Word enough that it is shaping the way we think, shaping the metaphors we use to understand life and the world. We organize our attitude by consciously choosing our speech and pruning our words. This goes both ways, too. We influence what we meditate on with what we say. We also influence what we talk about by what we think about.

We need bite-sized truths to percolate deep into our mind, not only broad, general reading. To meditate means to deliberate over, to ponder, to consider, to mull over. We can't really mull over chapters upon chapters at a time. We need to give ourselves small portions that will sink down deep, bit by bit.

One method of meditating on bite-sized pieces of truth enough to internalize them is using alignment cards. An alignment card is a verse, a motto, or a quote written out—usually on a sticky note or index card—and posted somewhere visible. Whenever you see the card, read it, pray it, and think about it. After dozens of repetitions, that bite-sized bit of truth will become a default thought planted firmly in your mind.

An alignment card is a simple, practical method to plant truth deep in the furrows of your heart and mind. It's particularly effective when you choose a Scripture to pray. My favorite places to put an alignment card prayer are on my bathroom mirror and on the window in front of the kitchen sink.

I also write a verse or quote on my weekly planner page and the front of my homeschool binder. If there's a spot you return to at least daily, especially during transitions in your day, it's a great place to stick an alignment card to tune your thoughts to truth.

The Truth Will Set You Free

When I first rolled up my sleeves as a young homemaker, I thought my job was to craft a family morning routine that would prevent spilled milk and broken dishes and maybe even all loud noises. I directed all my mental energy—but very little of my physical action—toward crafting a laundry routine that would keep the hampers empty and the laundry room clear.

Yet the loud noises continued, the oatmeal kept being smeared on the floors, and the laundry never stopped piling up, so I was obviously a failure at this whole homemaking thing. If I were a good homemaker, my home would always look and sound calm and beautiful, and there'd never be a backlog of laundry or dishes or crumbs.

I saw housework as a problem to be solved, so I felt caught in a hamster wheel, unable to escape because a solution never came. I kept hunting for the answer to something that wasn't a problem to be fixed but simply a duty to be done day after day. It wasn't my job to prevent the work from needing to be done but to do it as it needed doing. The problem was not the work; it was the story I was telling myself about the work.

These days, there are still times I look around and am tempted to think, "Woe is me! The house is a disaster again!" The blessings I count to drown out the self-pity and frustration are all the bustling activities that brought about the "disaster." I thank God for the opportunity to homeschool, for the children who have (messy) hobbies, for the people we were able to take a meal, for the books, for the weather and the gear it necessitates (whether swimsuits or snowsuits).

Sometimes, especially in our current house—a small, temporary rental—I think that I wouldn't be bothered by the gear if only I had a mud room so the boots and coats weren't shed in the living room. I think that if only I had more counter space or a bigger sink, then my kitchen wouldn't be so cluttered and cramped. Yet I know that we are where God wants us. I know He's actively working in my heart and my life, so I am to be satisfied in Him, regardless of my circumstances.

If the apostle Paul—who faced beatings and jail time—can learn to be content in whatever situation, then I, too, can learn to be content when my living room abounds with boots, coats, gloves, and scarves. Even this I can do through Him who strengthens me, knowing that it is the joy of the Lord that brings that strength. Where once I might have silently fumed, now I smile at the "disaster," which is just evidence of the abundance of life being lived in our home.

Take a Baby Step to Tell a Truer Story

Copy a Bible verse you want to make the focus of your thoughts onto an index card. Tape it to your bathroom mirror at eye level and pray it every time you stand there at the sink.

> *For the weapons of our warfare are not of the flesh but have divine power to destroy strongholds. We destroy arguments and every lofty opinion raised against the knowledge of God, and take every thought captive to obey Christ.*
>
> —2 Corinthians 10:4–5

8

Step 2: Tame Your Inner Toddler

The only kind of control we're supposed to have is self-control

> If you live for yourself, your comfort, your glory, your fame, you will miss out on your very purpose. God created you to bring glory to him.
>
> —Tim Challies, *Do More Better*

I had a toddler prone to tantrums. To this day, I am unsure what the trigger truly was. She would simply find something too much, so she'd collapse in a puddle of tears and sometimes screams, refusing both comfort and reason.

I felt helpless and clumsy while mothering her through her tantrums. But as I stood there, staring as she wallowed vocally in her distress, I realized that even though I did not scream and stomp, I was also a tantrum-thrower. I, too, wallowed in my distress when my folded laundry piles were overturned or when someone with dirty feet walked on my freshly mopped floor. Could my perception of my distress be just as overblown as my toddler's? Surely not.

If you've ever had to parent a toddler through a tantrum, you know it is no time to discuss reasonable arguments. Caught up in the emotional turmoil of the moment, the toddler can't even hear you. Our adult versions are the same.

I remember one internal tantrum I threw. I'd been reading some well-intentioned Christian advice to homemakers. On the one hand, I was looking for answers to guide my conscience on matters of housework. On the other hand, this source's logic was shallow. Feeling caught in a conundrum, I spiraled into a fussy fit.

Instead of being charitable, I construed the authors' argument in the worst possible manner. Apparently, I had to keep house because I was a woman. Someone has to do the boring, dirty work behind the scenes so that "real" work can be done elsewhere, and that's why God made women—as helpers, cleaning up after and feeding the men and their next generation.

Sure, without mothers, those men and the next generation wouldn't exist, but that didn't make the janitorial role more palatable to me. Did God really make women to do the cooking and cleaning and childbearing so that men would be free and able to accomplish things outside the home? Did God make women to be a subservient class?

Just like a fussy toddler, I was stubbornly immune to the fact the that my bad attitude was the root problem. Until I was willing to submit to God no matter what, giving up my fussy bad attitude even while I thought I was right, I had no chance of hearing reason, much less practicing it.

Finally, I sighed and said, "OK, God. Whatever you decide is fine with me. If you made me to be a janitor, I'll be a willing janitor." Only with a soft, obedient heart could I be given eyes to see how truncated my vision had been. Although homemaking might involve menial work, that does not make the role demeaning or subservient.

How can menial, service-oriented work be demeaning in a world where Jesus came as servant to all, washing feet and serving fish and bread? In the garden, before sin entered the world, man and woman were *both* given the job of tending the garden, improving its production.

It was only after I gave up my tantrum-like hardheartedness that I could begin to see, to *experience*, the goodness of God in designating homes as small outposts of the gospel in the midst of the world, dedicating a specially designed half of humanity to the maintenance thereof.

Nothing Ever Goes My Way!

At the root of most tantrums is an unmet desire. We encounter the limits of our ability or our resources or some other aspect of our finitude, and we don't like it. A tantrum—whether the dramatically audible version of a three-year-old or the quiet, martyr-like desperation typical of housewives—is anger at not getting our way. It is the opposite of a meek and quiet spirit, like Jesus's when He gave up the privileges of heaven and took on a human body with all its weakness.

The reality that three-year-olds are encountering for the first time—and adults still struggle with—is that life doesn't go our way, no matter how well or poorly we respond. No matter what we do, we are neither promised nor given an easy life. We can't find the perfect routine or perfect system and suddenly have all of life roll on smoothly without a hiccup.

That's not what we're about. We, like Jesus, are supposed to be about our Father's business: growing our people, reaching out to others, serving however we are being called here and now. Rough patches will come with that because that's how God strengthens us.

We will not always get our way, and we will be tempted to pitch a fit just like a three-year-old. Hard circumstances, however, are opportunities to rely on God rather than ourselves. Relying on this truth, we can find blessing in those circumstances. Difficult circumstances are not necessarily punishments or judgments; they can also be exercises given us to build our virtue and endurance.

How do we parent tantruming toddlers? We have to remain calm ourselves, setting the tone rather than descending to theirs. We have to hold the line of what is true and right, not allowing the toddler's emotions to control us. It's a kindness to not let someone's freak-out moment—whether that person is three or thirty—alter the direction. The adult maintains security and stability by holding the line of what is right, regardless of anyone's current emotional state.

So how do we parent *ourselves* when we are tempted to engage in an internal tantrum? We feel both the tension of the turbulent inner toddler and the voice of reason. Which will matter to us long-term? What is right in this moment? Which fork in the road will we follow—the path of the adult, choosing the long-term perspective, or the path of the toddler, indulging in momentary drama?

Notice the freak-out impulse, then take the deep breath you'd instruct your toddler to take. Don't freak out; just take care of whatever is in front of you. One reason we plan, write out our routines, and track our responsibilities is so that we are not left to our whims. The plan we make is our adult self giving our toddler-self clear instructions.

When we look at our plan at appropriate times, it can do its job: reminding us of what's on our plate. In order to work the plan, we have to listen to the planner self who made the plan rather than the in-the-moment self, who is too often like a spoiled toddler.

Don't let your self be your worst enemy. The planner self is the parent telling the toddler self, "No, first this." The more we practice self-discipline by obeying the planner-self and denying the toddler-self, the more mature we are going to act and become, and the more long-term satisfaction we will feel.

Sanctification Brings Self-Control

This is one of my favorite sayings for a reason: *The only kind of control you're supposed to have is self-control.* The fruit of the

The only kind of control you're supposed to have is self-control.

Spirit summarizes exactly what our attitudes should be. If you want to organize your attitude, you choose these attitudes to put on: love, joy, peace, patience, kindness, goodness, faithfulness, gentleness, self-control. It is a daunting list. We can't nail down a single one of them, much less all nine. But growing in them all is sanctification, which is God's will for us.

Sanctification is what homemaking is all about. Our duties provide us with opportunities to exercise the fruit of the Spirit. We mortify our default responses and choose to obey instead. We don't have to wallow in whatever comes naturally. That is acting like a toddler. Maturity is the ability and even the desire to do the right thing instead of what is easiest or more pleasurable in the moment.

We sometimes excuse our wallowing, our tantrums, by calling them authentic and honest. However, we don't need to be authentic versions of *ourselves* as much as we need to be authentic *followers of Jesus*. Being an authentic follower of Jesus means choosing His mind rather than our own, His glory rather than our pride.

After all, it is only because of Jesus that we can choose the right mindset in the first place. Jesus pours out His Holy Spirit, and the Holy Spirit brings the fruit. The fruit of the Spirit—self-control included—are not responses we have to manufacture on our own steam, because *we can't*. They are responses given to us by grace that we can walk in and grow up into.

The Heidelberg Catechism, written by Dutch Protestants in 1563, says, "God gives His grace and Holy Spirit only to those who pray continually and groan inwardly, asking God for these gifts and thanking Him for them." A prayer asking for the fruit of the Spirit is a prayer God will answer. This is how we get the grace to do the right thing in the middle of the muddling. No matter how much we get organized, life will always be outside our control. However, our response to life—our attitude—is fully under our control.

Have you ever noticed your ability to turn on a different persona, a different response to life, at least momentarily, when you open the door or answer the phone? This shows us we have the ability to exhibit self-control. Too often, our tone and tactics with our kids do not demonstrate such control. When we jump on them, pester and harp, and then switch it off immediately if someone walks in the door, we've got a clue—there's a problem.

The fact that we can exercise self-control when we're sufficiently motivated can at least give us hope. It shows us it's possible. We simply need to take that start and extend it farther. We don't have to wait for the doorbell to ring unexpectedly in order to put on a cheerful face. We can do it as soon as the Spirit nudges us that we're being fussy.

We don't have to be trapped by the whims of our moods. We can be well-parented, cheerful, civilized toddlers because our Father is the best Father, Who loves us and trains us while giving us the grace to obey. We can choose our attitudes, repent of our whining, and cheer up

> We can choose our attitudes, repent of our whining, and cheer up because God gives us the grace and strength to do so.

because God gives us the grace and strength to do so.

Growth Takes Time

When we work at organization, we're generally hunting for more personal peace, fulfillment, enjoyment, and strength. All these come when we follow basic personal stewardship practices. In fact, the most common self-care activities used to be called "disciplines." They were merely a part of being ready, in season and out, to serve faithfully.

Discipline does not always seem pleasant in the moment, but afterward, it brings sweet fruit to those who have submitted to it. Just like fussy, grabby toddlers, we have inner voices and desires that need discipline. We know how to parent, and we can turn that parenting attention to our own selves.

More important than making your two-year-old eat broccoli is making yourself eat well. More important than stopping a two-year-old tantrum-in-progress is stopping—or better yet, preventing—a tantrum of your own, whether the tantrum is internal, pouty and sulky, or expressed in more socially nuanced and acceptable ways.

Fruit doesn't appear overnight on a tree, though. Toddlers remain in our home for discipline for well over a decade because that's how long it takes. Discipline grows over time and then must ripen. Likewise, our fruit isn't instantaneous in its development or in its worthiness. Making a decision to plant some seeds won't slingshot you into harvest. Impatience—like Frog yelling at his seeds to START GROWING—won't help.

Patience buds and develops when toddlers are spilling milk and breaking dishes and then walking through the mess, unaware. Patience keeps at table manners and good habits for years after we thought we'd get the payoff of "smooth and easy days." Patience doesn't look for a fully ripened fruit before its time. It is willing to stick out the long growing season and does not doubt that the ripening and harvest will come.

Every act of patience is a drop of sap helping to grow our fruit. Our children are baby trees of their own, not the fruit on our tree. We're in the same orchard together, but the fruit we must be looking to increase is the fruit of the Spirit within our own lives. They, too, will grow the same fruits through the Spirit's work in them.

Growing Up into Follow-Through

Our routines provide a basic, daily opportunity to parent our own inner two-year-old, to put to death the indulgence of the moment and do the responsible, right thing. It's about so much more than toilets or dust. It's about becoming a person of follow-through.

Follow-through isn't necessarily an inborn ability or a personality trait. It's a habit that's been built up by repeated practice over years. Most women who have it, for whom it appears natural, began forming the habit in childhood. For those of us who did not form the habit of follow-through as children, there is still hope—but we won't be zapped with the ability to reliably follow through on our tasks simply by designing a great routine on paper. Instead, we build our ability over time.

We're used to being motivated by excitement, by inspiration. Commercials are loud, bright, and over-the-top because excitement is the easy button when it comes to motivation. After decades of media consumption, we're accustomed to having our easy button pressed. On top of that, prizes and rewards—treats, sugar, and fun toys–were probably used most of our childhood to motivate us to do well.

Chores are not glitzy, bright, fun, or sweet. So, like spoiled toddlers, we struggle to find inspiration or motivation to complete them. Cultures that are better about routines and regularity find duty to be a motivating factor. Such societies teach their young that duty is inspiring. Modern Americans, on the other hand, have been told duty is oppressive, so it's no wonder that stability-giving habits are difficult for us.

We can't undo our culture, our enculturation, or our upbringing, but we *can* start down a new path. We start by acknowledging that the easy button won't happen here. Even the routines themselves, once in place, aren't an easy button. We have to continually remind ourselves that virtue is rewarding, even if it isn't fun or sweet.

Laughing at My Toddler Self

When I had three small children, I took their offenses too seriously. I had friends who would recount the messy, irresponsible antics of their children while doubled over in laughter, and I couldn't relate. What I saw was the resulting extra work. I saw how far from perfect my children were, and I thought my job was shuffling them toward perfection—so their childlike antics were also my parenting failures.

Looking back, I'm not surprised by my tendency as a young mom. I had always wanted to be a grown-up. I felt like I had finally arrived when I turned twenty, even though I'd already been married a year. By the time I was twenty-five, I had three kids, yet I still felt like I was playing maturity catch-up with those around me.

Now, looking back—past forty—I know I was playing maturity catch-up because maturity isn't a function of taking myself seriously. Taking myself too seriously got in the way of my maturity and sanctification. Like a child, I pictured adulthood as importance, as having it all together, so that's what I tried to achieve.

Adulthood, however, is about having the responsibility and maturity to do the right thing whether you feel like it or not. Adulthood is playing the long game, acting according to the big picture without getting sidetracked by fleeting distractions.

The more experience, maturity, and sanctification I gain, the less seriously I take myself. Not surprisingly, I can get a lot more

The more experience, maturity, and sanctification I gain, the less seriously I take myself.

done because I'm not getting in my own way with second-guessing and hissy fits. We can laugh at things in movies or stories that we would not laugh at in our own life because we have distance from the situation. But if we experience stress, fear, or obligation when encountering a surprise in our own life, it's much harder to laugh about it. Life is full of surprises. When we can find a way to laugh instead of moan, complain, or worry, we will be mentally and emotionally healthier for it.

Take a Baby Step to Parent Yourself

Give your routines or tedious tasks an amusing, catchy name and use it a lot. Want the kids to wipe out the sink after they brush their teeth? Want to do that yourself? Call it "Spit and Shine." Need to start folding laundry, but you're always reluctant? Call it "Learning with Laundry" and listen to a podcast, online course, or audiobook while you fold.

> *It is for discipline that you have to endure. God is treating you as sons. For what son is there whom his father does not discipline? If you are left without discipline, in which all have participated, then you are illegitimate children and not sons . . . For the moment all discipline seems painful rather than pleasant, but later it yields the peaceful fruit of righteousness to those who have been trained by it.*
>
> —Hebrews 12:7–8, 11

9

Step 3: Take Baby Steps

We can't do it all, and we shouldn't pretend that someday we will

Let us be on the watch for opportunities of usefulness; let us go about the world with our ears and our eyes open, ready to avail ourselves of every occasion for doing good; let us not be content till we are useful, but make this the main design and ambition of our lives.

—Charles Spurgeon

Our dining room chairs had fabric seats that had seen better days. The beige canvas had splotches of pink, stains of coffee, discolorations from unknown sources. The chairs were unappealing. I wanted to recover the seats, and I put it on my list week after week. It never happened. The closest I got was browsing the fabric store and confirming that, yes, I could do this, and there was fabric to choose from.

I had no idea how much fabric to buy. I didn't know how the seats attached to the chairs. I wasn't sure if one used glue or something else to attach the new fabric. Do you remove the old or let it sit and fester underneath? Honestly, I had no idea how to proceed, but reupholstering was something normal people did, which meant I could probably figure it out, so I put it on my list.

After two or three months of listing this project and yet doing nothing, I realized I was going to have to do something other than just put it on my list. I had listed the project as if it were a single task. What was the first task, really? Well, I needed to know how much fabric to buy. That meant measuring and doing some math.

So that week, instead of writing "Reupholster dining room chairs," I wrote "Measure chair seats and calculate fabric yardage" on my list. And then I did it! While I was measuring, I also took a closer look at the chairs and discovered how the seat was attached to the base. I then located the kind of screwdriver I needed in order to take the chairs apart.

The next week, I wrote, "Buy fabric for chairs," on my list, and while I was out running errands, I did! When I got the fabric home, I went ahead and cut it into squares. I wondered if I'd be able to take the chairs apart on my own, so I tried the screwdriver on one. I was just checking, not trying to get the whole job done. It turned out it was easy. Not only that, but I also saw on the underside of the seat that the original fabric was stapled on. I had another question answered.

The next day, I borrowed a staple gun from a friend, took all the chairs apart, stapled my new fabric squares to the seats, and scrubbed down the seat bases while I was so up-close-and-personal with them. They were pretty grody. I was still occupied with screwing the freshly reupholstered seats into the bases when my husband came home. "Oh," he said, "you should use a drill for that." He grabbed his drill and finished reattaching the seats for me in no time.

A job I had procrastinated doing for months turned out to be no big deal. I fit it into the nooks and crannies of two regular weeks, with no long stretches of time required. What made the difference? Instead of treating the multi-step project as a single task on my list, I figured out the next small step. Once I started on a small task, I ended up making progress beyond what I'd planned, whereas I never even got started when the daunting whole was on my list.

I'm Too Old for Baby Steps!

Often, the time we spend researching or brainstorming new systems is actually time spent trying to find a substitute for doing the work. We want a system that, once in place, will make life easy. Or we spend our time figuring out the very best way to do something because we're focused on creating something impressive or being someone impressive.

As adults, we want our steps to be smooth, suave, and sizable. So we end up not taking any steps at all because we're afraid we'll fall. We need to be more like babies. Baby steps are a way to begin in humility, recognizing that we can only take moment-by-moment steps of faith and faithfulness. We move forward, satisfied with the work of the day, even if we didn't achieve grand results.

Baby steps are an appropriate name for small tasks not only because of their relative size, but also because we, as mothers, can easily picture the early stage of learning to walk. We don't expect a one-year-old to be running marathons. We don't expect him to keep up with teenage brothers.

Yet, as mothers, we are thrilled with each little toddle. We celebrate. We applaud and cheer and coax him to take just one more step. Strength and confidence grow one toddle at a time, until walking becomes automatic. At first, each step is a grand achievement on its own, to be recognized and celebrated.

Humility helps us take the posture of a small child, even in areas where we think we should already be marathon runners. If we aren't there yet, we can't let our pride get in the way of learning to walk. Comparing ourselves to others makes as much sense as a sixteen-month-old refusing to walk at all because a ten-month-old friend is already steady on his feet.

Infants learning to walk will fall down. If falling down was evidence of an inability to walk, none of us would ever have become walkers. We all fell while learning. Then we got up and tried again. No one remembers how many times we repeated this process. We only know that we mastered the process of putting one foot in front of the other because we didn't stop trying when we lost our balance along the way.

In the same way, dropping balls around the house, messing up our routines, and losing our momentum are instances of falling over that have no bearing on our potential for the future. None of these scenarios mean we aren't making progress. The next step is to get back up and try again.

We fight baby steps, though. We want to just be done already. We don't want to take the time or admit we need to take the time. We are too proud for baby steps. We want instant gratification for our goals and projects.

Fighting against baby steps is choosing perfectionism and procrastination. Instead, we need to remember:

Some is better than none.
Make it better, not perfect.
Progress over perfection.

The point of our work at home is never to complete everything all at once, but to continuously do something to make life better. Choose baby steps to make real progress. Progress doesn't come after we've figured out the perfect system. Progress comes one step at a time.

Momentum Comes by Baby Steps

We need to break the huge project down, not only into a doable step, but into a very small step so we can just get started. Load the dishwasher. Swish the toilet. Dust the mantel. Spot-mop the kitchen. Spend five minutes tidying up the bedroom floors. Start a load of laundry. As we take these kinds of small steps, we find that they lead to momentum rather than the boom-and-bust cycle we're used to.

When a task is so small that it's not intimidating, we experience a win we never get when we set our hopes on "finishing" the job. One win leads to another. We're willing to take another small step because we know we can, and we see that we will appreciate the effect. Momentum and meaningful management start with baby steps.

Baby steps are actions that are simple to start and quick to complete. Baby steps do not get a job done, but they do move it forward. Our perfectionism will rear all its ugly complaints and modes of resistance when we try a baby step, but if we listen, we'll be stuck in overwhelm and despondency or wishful future-thinking.

Baby steps, one after another, add up to much more than you'd ever expect if you looked at only one on a list and considered it alone. No baby step on its own is very significant. However, because they prompt action and carry momentum, baby steps are much more effective than any grand plan or perfect system.

When we begin to take action more consistently, a weird thing happens with our time. Even though we do more, we have more time. If you feel like there's too much to do and you need to cut back, try cutting back on the internal whining first. Make a list, choose one thing that will make a difference, and spend ten minutes doing it. Ten minutes is enough time to make progress, but it's also super easy to blink and have ten minutes disappear. When we become more accustomed to using our ten minutes productively, in directing them intentionally, we discover that we do, indeed, have plenty of time to do what's important.

Begin by gathering everything that nags you by jotting it down—this is a brain dump. Once you have all the things that require your attention gathered in one place, you'll automatically feel calmer and more focused because your mental energy has been freed from the burden of remembering everything you're stressed about. You'll be amazed at how much this simple practice uncovers your thinking patterns and allows you to address them directly.

Working with Humility

Our goals are big. We basically want to be a different kind of person than we are. Perhaps we want to be a person who prays for an hour, but right now we never pause to pray at all. Perhaps we want to be thin or fit or strong, but right now we are not. Perhaps we want to be the sort of person who follows through on our plans, but right now we're more likely to bury our head in our phone than deal with our well-intentioned plan.

James Clear, in *Atomic Habits*, writes: "Life goals are good to have because they provide direction, but they can also trick you into taking on more than you can handle. Daily habits—tiny routines that are repeatable—are what make big dreams a reality."

We do have big dreams for lasting personal change, and we know we can only get there a step at a time, but the steps seem so insignificant that they aren't worth bothering with. So we procrastinate, distract, stay stuck, or drift even farther from our ideal.

You know you won't be a whole new person overnight, so don't try. But keep the vision, because knowing where you're headed helps keep you on the path. Building small habits truly will move you toward your vision.

Change happens incrementally, not overnight. Build slowly, and the lifestyle change will grow and flourish, taking root in a more lasting and meaningful way than an overnight installation of a whole new lifestyle. Stick with the small changes. You're neither too good for them nor too far gone. They are meaningful. They don't devalue or deny the vision. Instead, they are the means to get you there, step by step.

> Change happens incrementally, not overnight.

Focus on What Matters Day by Day

Baby steps might seem overwhelming at first because our to-do list has the potential to triple or quadruple if we break down our projects into doable steps. It's easy to get lost in a sea—or swamp—of seemingly unending tasks. That's why we have to get radical with our baby steps and start making a mini to-do list every day.

Every day, I make a new to-do list—just for that day—on a sticky note. With such limited space, I'm forced to keep my to-do list short, which is another way of keeping it realistic. Because we are limited—in time, in resources, in energy—our to-do list also needs to be limited.

Routines (covered in chapter 11) are one way to use our time and attention wisely, but there is always more to do than the basic housekeeping routines. Most of us have a long laundry list—whether mental or written—filled to overflowing with tasks and projects we could, should, or would be doing. Using a sticky note or index card to make a daily plan helps us remember that not only our time, but also our energy, attention, and abilities are limited—so we should plan accordingly.

I'm not talking about cramming a full to-do list in minuscule print on a sticky note, either. Our daily to-do list should be a list of the *three* most important things. Of all the things you will do and want to do, what will count as sufficient for the day? If you do your chosen three tasks, you get to—and ought to—count the day as a win.

You will, of course, do more in a day than the three things written down on your daily card, but if you start with what's most important, you'll feel better about how you've used your time. You'll probably also get more done in the long run because you're focused and clear rather than scattered and stressed. You'll see that you're spending your time well.

A daily card with your three top tasks offers plenty of flexibility, even for those who are busy, Type-A, high-energy moms, spinning multiple plates daily. It works just as well for laid-back, spontaneous types. When we identify what's most important, write it down, and make our note-to-self visible, we are more likely to follow through on those items, no matter what our personality type.

The daily to-do list reminds us by its very nature to focus on priorities and not to overestimate what we're able to do. It forces us to baby-step-size our expectations. Each day, we can take stock of our family's needs, our energy, and our most pressing obligations, then use our to-do list to put first things first.

Some days, this might mean project tasks while other days it means completing the homeschool day and no more. Some days it means setting the list aside and dealing with an emergency. Every day, we evaluate and make the best intentional choices we can. The limit of three tasks reminds us of our finitude. We cannot do all we want to do. We need a to-do list, not a *want-to-do* list. Choosing three tasks forces us to prioritize and focus on what *needs* to be done rather than what we *wish* we could do.

> Every day, we evaluate and make the best intentional choices we can.

For example, I have task lists scattered everywhere: a task app, my planner, Evernote, sticky notes, and in purple notebooks all around my house. If I was trying to keep all those tasks in mind, I'd go crazy. But they're written down so that I don't have to keep them in mind. What's most important is on my daily card so I don't have to check all those scattered lists, either.

I might want to derail my day and choose to work on a project that's more appealing or seems more urgent. I remember one day when I felt a wild hair coming on that I really needed to empty out, clean, and reorganize the pantry closet. But my daily card said (1) homeschool, (2) record podcast, and (3) take meal. So I had to either have those three things taken care of before I started on the pantry *or* I had to decide the pantry was more important than my obligation to take a meal, show up on time for a podcast recording, and educate my kids.

Instead of touching the pantry, I wrote it down as a potential project for another day in my task app. Because it was written down, I had done something about it, and I wasn't worried I'd forget that it really did need to be tackled. It took three weeks before I finally got to the pantry project, but when I did, it was because I had the margin for it, and I wasn't dropping my true priorities in favor of a whim to accomplish a small makeover.

A daily card with a top three to-do list also helps us choose and notice our real wins. When we're working to increase our effectiveness, it's important to see progress rather than failure. Too often, we only notice what we *didn't* do in a day, which brings down our attitude and energy. When we complete our list of three, we are forced to recognize that we did what needed to be done. We're able to call it a good day and end it satisfied.

Take a Baby Step to Do What Matters

Choose three important things that must be done today. Write the date and day of the week at the top of a sticky note or index card, then list your top three. Try again tomorrow.

> *I appeal to you therefore, brothers, by the mercies of God, to present your bodies bas a living sacrifice, holy and acceptable to God, which is your spiritual worship . . . Let love be genuine. Abhor what is evil; hold fast to what is good. Love one another with brotherly affection. Outdo one another in showing honor. Do not be slothful in zeal, be fervent in spirit, serve the Lord. Rejoice in hope, be patient in tribulation, be constant in prayer. Contribute to the needs of the saints and seek to show hospitality.*
>
> —Romans 12:1, 9–13

10

Step 4: Invest Your Time

Time is a gift God gives us
to render back to Him in grateful praise

> Your goal is not to stick to a given schedule at all costs; it's instead to maintain, at all times, a thoughtful say in what you're doing with your time going forward.
>
> — Cal Newport, *Deep Work*

I was driving the kids home from piano lessons at three in the afternoon. As I maneuvered around the roundabout, it suddenly flashed into my mind that, the week prior, I had signed up to take a meal to a church family, and I hadn't written it down. When was I supposed to take them dinner? Thursday. What day was it? Thursday!

In two hours, I was supposed to be showing up on their doorstep with a hot and ready meal. My mind reeled. Yes, I did consider pizza. I don't remember what I ended up making, but as soon as I got home, I was able to whip something up—*sans* dessert—and arrive on time as if I hadn't forgotten.

Write it down, right away. I tell myself this all the time for good reason. Whenever I don't, I regret it.

Like the time I made well-child appointments for two or three children over the phone. I looked at the calendar while making them. The timing would work great. But I didn't note them down right away. I saw the time. I knew the time. I'd write it down later.

I'm not even sure what it was I did before writing those appointments on my calendar. I did end up writing something down, but I got the time wrong. Standing at the check-in counter weeks later, I remember being told I was an hour late, and they wouldn't be able to see the kids. I could reschedule.

Mortified, I rescheduled right then and there at the receptionist's desk, and I entered the new appointment into my calendar, verbally double-checking the day and time. We arrived at that appointment just fine, without hassle or drama.

Ever since then, whenever I stand at a doctor's or dentist's or orthodontist's check-in counter, I don't take the handwritten appointment card they offer. Instead, I put the appointment in my digital calendar on my phone right away, confirming both day and time as I do.

If you want to be organized, *write it down, right away, every time.*

Tell Me All the Time Management Secrets

I'm sorry to break the news to you: There is no such thing as time management. There's only self-management. You don't use your time better and end up with more, though there are things we can do to maximize our use of the time we have.

> **There is no such thing as time management. There's only self-management.**

If you feel like you don't have enough time to do all the things on your list, you're correct. Nothing is wrong with you. It's simply true. We don't have enough time to do everything we'd like to do. Time is not something we can control, manipulate, or change. Nothing we do will create more time, but there's a lot we can do to use the time we have well, stewarding it and making the most of it.

If we try to use time management strategies, tips, or techniques that assume we have control over our time and control over all the things we need to do, then we're going to end up frustrated—not because we're doing anything wrong, either; we're simply coming at our life from the wrong perspective, with the wrong expectations.

As mothers, we are caretakers, which means our time is not our own to use at our discretion and arrange as we please. We have to remain flexible and responsive in order to mother well. Because raising our children is our top priority, they are not interruptions. They aren't getting in the way of our work when they need us. They—and their needs—*are* the work.

It's easy to see our children's needs as something we have to get out of the way before we can do the things we need to do. Our biggest time management hurdle is not arranging our life so that we can accomplish our to-do list, but rather, arranging our to-do list so that we can pay attention to our life.

Time management is not about making the right tweaks so that everything we want fits into our day. If that's our goal, we're always going to be hunting for the secret sauce or the magic formula that will make our personal pet plans happen.

The definition of good time management isn't doing all the things on our list; it's doing what we're called to do. When we see that our time is taken up with our duties, we can happily get busy with those duties. We can keep our head in the game, do our work with a cheerful goodwill, and be sanctified by it.

The definition of good time management isn't doing all the things on our list; it's doing what we're called to do.

We're giving up the wishful thinking, giving up the total life overhauls, and giving up trying to make life go our way; instead, we're looking at what we are actually responsible for and making those things our priorities, cheerfully choosing them day in and day out.

Include a Day of Rest on Your Calendar

Here we are, mothers of bustling families, running around like crazies all week, wishing for time off or a day out, and mentally griping about the amount of work we have. Sunday comes, the Ten Commandments are read, and we think, *Well, God didn't actually mean that one about Sabbath. There's no way I can take a day off every week.*

Sure enough, the thing you know you need is exactly the thing God has made provision for. But instead of receiving it joyfully, we reenact the Israelites' wanderings in the desert, saying God's provision isn't good enough because it isn't what we would have picked.

Taking a day off is very clear-cut for people with a career outside the home. They don't go into the office. It's a home day. Good for them. What if all days are home days? What if the home *is* your work? What if you're surrounded by your work everywhere you turn? How can we take Sunday off, right smack in the middle of everything that needs to be done, and while people still insist on eating and making messes?

We do it by faith in Christ. In Christ, we can rest, even when the house is falling down around us. Even when the to-do list is still a mile long, if Christ says to us, "Hey, today, just stop; find your rest in Me" why wouldn't we?

It turns out we wouldn't. It turns out we're like the Israelites. God says there'll be enough manna for the Sabbath, but we don't gather extra and then complain when the manna doesn't show up. God says He'll take care of us, but we aren't so sure because it doesn't look the way we want it to look. We want a day of rest made in our own image.

Yes, a Sabbath should be a day of rest, but we tend to start with our own expectations instead of with faith. We want the day to look like our version of rest. We want the house to be clean and calm and peaceful. In fact, we demand that it must be before we make it a day of rest, so we scramble and scramble and never get there.

True rest is by faith, not by sight. It is obeying first, trusting that God will come through and make it all work. Maybe I don't need to understand what perfect obedience looks like before I begin. After all, Christ is my perfect obedience.

Instead, I can take a small first step. I can say, "You know, on Sunday, I won't care about the state of the kids' rooms, and I won't make a to-do list, and I won't think about homeschooling." Instead of trying to start with a total day of rest, perfectly out of the gate, start with the obvious and grow gradually from there.

The Sabbath is a day assigned to stop our striving to get ahead and remember that every good gift comes from God, not our own efforts. If we take one day out of seven away from work, we'll find we return to our daily life better equipped and more energetic. We will better use the time we have after taking one day off. Come Monday, when the work is still there, I can dig in. I've rested. I can do what needs to be done with energy instead of resentment, with joy instead of bitterness and fatigue.

It's not that the work disappears or that I'm earning a reward for obeying God's Law. Starting the week with a day of rest is a tangible, visible practice of offering to God the first fruits of my time and trusting Him for my needs—including trust for Monday morning cheerfulness and energy. When the Lord's Day is prioritized and taken in faith, those Martha jobs on Monday are not fretful and fussy but joyful service, informed by Mary's focus.

Thinking of Time in Intervals

Once, trying to lose the baby weight, I tried the Couch to 5K running program—a nine-week interval training program that moves you from running only one minute at a time to running thirty minutes. While I was trying to get into shape, I was also trying to get my home into shape. What can I say? It was the "My baby is nearly a year old, and I really need to get my act together" phase. Been there? I've been there five times.

As I was huffing and puffing up the sidewalk one day, I connected the dots between an accountability-productivity model (agile) my husband's company uses, my six-week school terms, and interval running. Programmers use agile development because it allows them to iterate, working with the current situation, program, and requirements rather than assuming they can predict what will be both needed five years down the road when a "complete" product might be feasible.

Similarly, with interval training, you slowly build up stamina by going all-out for a short time, then resting, then pushing again, then resting again. I realized I could use the same principles to improve my housekeeping, as well. An interval became the amount of time I could wrap my head around and plan for—about six weeks. Anything beyond six weeks went onto a "someday/maybe" list. I kept my eyes on what was in front of me: the habit or routine I was trying to build, the birthday to plan next month, the decluttering I was making progress toward.

Intervals are the key to a mindset shift that allows us to move forward toward our goals in bite-size, reasonable iterations rather than waiting for the stars to align or for our motivation to pull us together. It's a grid to be realistic about our time and put some blinders on in order to focus just on the next steps. It's a way to be aware of current commitments and accept them rather than procrastinate.

The Weekly Review Is Your Investment Manager

Flying by the seat of our pants is not a method for investing time intentionally and effectively. We often choose "spontaneity" as a method because our plans never seem to work out, and we assume the time spent planning was wasted.

Maybe it was. Too often, our plans are wishful thinking on paper, not preparation for our real life. Instead, we need to make plans in light of our current reality, using them not as a tool of control against others, but as a tool to control our own moment-by-moment choices, even if the moment's choice is to switch gears and take care of an urgent, unexpected need.

Our plans should help us make on-the-spot judgment calls with calm clarity and consistent conviction. The weekly review is a time set aside to remember what we have on our plates and choose our commitments so we can stay organized.

Our plans should help us make on-the-spot judgment calls with calm clarity and consistent conviction.

We take some time and look at the calendar, make fresh to-do lists, decide what our biggest responsibilities are this week, and then make sure those stay in front of us so they can get done. A weekly review is the key to staying on top of the maintenance real life requires.

Moms need a weekly review just as much as a business executive. We have sports practices, volunteer dates, meals, and so much more we must accomplish in a week. The process of evaluating everything that's coming up in a calm manner beforehand helps us meet our commitments with peace and preparedness.

Regular review is the absolute key to maintaining a sense of organization. We have to look at our lists to make them happen, and that looking over is called a review. A weekly review sharpens our intuitive focus on important projects as we deal with the flood of new input and potential distractions coming at us the rest of the week.

If we have a sense of where we are, where we're going, and what we have going on, we'll be able to make better on-the-fly decisions about commitments and responsibilities and ideas that come at us throughout the week. That's one way we stay organized.

It can be hard to discipline ourselves to set aside the time for a weekly review. We're used to scrambling. We just keep on going as one week becomes another without pausing to reflect and set ourselves up for any solid, focused progress. But it's our own peace of mind and sanity we are sacrificing when we skip a weekly review.

In his productivity classic, *Getting Things Done*, David Allen says that a weekly review is the key to both peace of mind and staying organized. His version requires two hours on Friday, but we're going to adopt the baby step version and iterate slowly, only adding what we actually need.

Start your weekly review routine with fifteen minutes to prepare for the week ahead. A weekly review is the key, the linchpin, to ensuring that our plans are effective and helpful, not a waste of time. It is by a regular weekly review that we can keep a clear mind and a sense of relaxed control in the midst of a busy and full life.

It is precisely because our work at home threatens to deluge and overwhelm us at all hours every day that we need to carve out a time and space to strategize, to regroup, and to be refreshed. Our difficulty is not in finding fifteen minutes for such a review. The difficulty is in choosing to use it for a weekly review instead of zoning out on random internet searches, Amazon-browsing, or social media scrolling.

We must be both savvy and disciplined enough to know the value of sacrificing fake relaxation for the truly refreshing and rejuvenating option. As moms, we're functioning as managers of our homes. If we want to be effective, we will take the time to keep up-to-date and on top of our game. We can't do that moment by moment, so we must carve out fifteen minutes or so at the end of the week to pull back and process.

We must carve out fifteen minutes or so at the end of the week to pull back and process.

Life Isn't Color-Coded

I can't count how many planners I have either made or purchased. With most of them, I spent more time creating one and setting it up than I did actually using it. That is, I spent more time dreaming than doing.

I could have learned this lesson sooner. I once had a friend who had the most effective planner I had ever seen, but it took me years to follow her example. I had never known anyone who used a planner the way she used hers. It was only a spiral notebook. It was cheap. It was unadorned. It was ragged. It was scrappy. It worked.

Her family had just moved halfway across the country with a passel of small children. They landed at our church, and she started coming to our weekly playgroup. Her spiral notebook was always within her reach. It was her brain on paper. She had a lot to keep track of, so she wrote down as much as she could. She kept it up with no rhyme or reason, no stickers, no headings or index or apparent organization.

When she knew she'd need to remember something, she wrote it on the next available line. When she needed to make a list, she started it on the next available line. When she needed to find something, she flipped through her pages and scanned until she found it. She was unassuming and brilliant, and I didn't appreciate it until years later, after dozens of failed planner attempts.

I thought that if something so simple would work, how much better would it be if it had a little structure, a little beauty, a little pizzazz? Not better at all. What makes a planner of any kind work is *using it*: writing things down and then referencing what you wrote. If you do that, your planner works, no matter how incomplete, incoherent, and scrappy.

Maybe it was the scrappy element that made it work. Pretty planners can be intimidating. We want our life to be as pretty and as comprehensively outlined as the planner itself. The planner is where we retreat to escape our real life, to pretend we are prepared for all the things. When the day dawns, we avoid the planner and just hit the ground running because our life doesn't fit the planner's illusory structure.

I do use a printed planner, but I try to use it the way my friend used her spiral notebook, and I know my habits could transfer to a spiral notebook if that's all that was available. Every week has blank days, days I didn't end up making a plan. But every week also has, scattered about, notes to myself that I browse back over. I know if I write it down in my planner, I will see it. It won't fall through the cracks—not because the planner itself is doing any work, but because I write things down, then look over them regularly.

Some days need to be more planned than others, so thinking every day should have the same formatted plan is unrealistic. Perhaps it's not consistency—doing the same thing every time—that we need, so much as gradually increasing our follow-through. Follow-through is gained by practice—not unbroken streaks but increasing repetitions. The more we do something, the easier it becomes to do still more.

Our time isn't our own to decorate the way we want, arranging it just so to get the right effect. Our time is a limited resource, and we will be satisfied in how we spent our days only if we spent them not daydreaming about getting in control, but rolling up our sleeves and digging into the good works God has put in front of us to do.

We will be satisfied in how we spent our days only if we spent them not daydreaming about getting in control, but rolling up our sleeves and digging into the good works God has put in front of us to do.

Take a Baby Step to Invest Your Time

Set a timer and spend fifteen minutes preparing yourself for the coming week. During your fifteen-minute weekly review, look over your calendar for the next two weeks, taking notes about how best to prepare for what's ahead. Prepare a fresh routine checklist and task list for the next week, moving over the things that didn't happen last week. Take some notes about meals or groceries based on your activities this week, even if it's not a complete menu plan. When your fifteen minutes are up, remember that some is better than none.

> *He who supplies seed to the sower and bread for food will supply and multiply your seed for sowing and increase the harvest of your righteousness. You will be enriched in every way to be generous in every way, which through us will produce thanksgiving to God.*
>
> —2 Corinthians 9:10–11

11

Step 5: Establish Small Routines

Routines don't have to be perfect to be helpful

> The way you keep your house, the way you organize your time, the care you take in your personal appearance, the things you spend your money on, all speak loudly about what you believe. The beauty of thy peace shines forth in an ordered life. A disordered life speaks loudly of disorder in the soul.
>
> —Elisabeth Elliot, *Let Me Be a Woman*

I knocked tentatively on the door of my friend's house. I had something to drop off, and she had said she might not be home, or she might be upstairs nursing. She had given me permission to just walk in and leave it on her entryway table if she didn't answer.

We both had three small children, from infant to preschool-age. I'd been to her house before, but only for group playdates or dinners—the kind of planned event you clean house for. She didn't answer my knock, so I slowly turned the knob and peered inside. It was quiet. No one was around.

There were some blankets on the floor, perhaps dropped by the toddler having a dance party before leaving. There were miscellaneous items on the entryway table, just like at my house. I don't know what I was expecting, but I felt startled by the state of her house. Honestly, she had left it more tidied up than I had left mine, but I'd never seen it when it wasn't company-ready.

I realized that, for some reason, I had assumed she didn't work for that tidied-up state—not like I did, anyway. I assumed her house was always neat because I had never seen it otherwise. *Some people are like that,* I had thought, *just naturally clean, so messes hardly even happen.*

When I opened her door, I expected to see a house that was company-ready, not a house that had seen action all morning before a mom with three small children had to be off somewhere. So when I saw her home in still-life, as it were, I suddenly felt at ease. I felt a new connection with this friend who wasn't even present.

We're in this together. We're all managing busy, active households and trying to keep up with the life being lived. The goal isn't for our house to be in a perfect state, but for us to keep everything and everyone functioning and moving forward. Sometimes that happens less consistently, but we stick with it, not trying to maintain company-clean every minute of every day.

The System Isn't the Secret

Housework is never done. We make the checkmark, but the task returns the very next day or week—maybe even the same day or hour. Our goal can't be to "finish" the housework or "complete" our chores, but rather to put in the repetitions, to do the time.

Rather than reaching for finality and perfection, our goal ought to be regularity, a daily "good enough." The daily good enough— not the daily best or daily perfect end result—then becomes our routine.

The dictionary says that a routine is "a sequence of actions regularly followed." Notice the grace built into that definition. "Regularly followed" doesn't require "followed every single day without fail at exactly the same time."

The dictionary also calls a routine a "fixed program." The checklist of chores we need to regularly repeat is our program. We open it up, look at it, and use that information to direct our next steps. We know what's next because it's in the program. We make the program a routine by regularly following it.

Rather than reaching for finality and perfection, our goal ought to be regularity, a daily "good enough."

But what is your program trying to accomplish? What is a clean (or clean enough) home? It seems like it should be possible to keep a decent and orderly home, doesn't it? Or is it simply impossible, especially with young children?

Yes and no.

Think about what you mean by "clean house" when you say that phrase to yourself. Picture what you want. Look around at your current reality. If "clean house" conjures up pictures of completely empty counters, decorated bookshelves, never-smudged windows, and spotless floors, then you are setting yourself up for frustration and failure.

If "clean house" means "functioning house," however, we have a useful definition. Our homes are tools to be used for the real goal of loving our families and serving the people God brings through our door as well as the people we meet when we go out the door. The goal is not to have a home that is clean for its own sake. A home that is clean but serving no one is barren, wasted, useless.

> A home that is clean but serving no one is barren, wasted, useless.

A dirty, chaotic home is not a useful tool, either. If we can never find what we need, if our bathrooms can't welcome a visitor, if no one has clean clothes to wear out of the house, then we aren't stewarding our resources to anywhere near their potential.

Every homemaker needs to decide what "reasonably clean" is *for her house*. We each must find our balance between "my household can function smoothly" and "cleaning is stressing me out because it's undone every time a child walks through a room." We don't want to be a frazzled mess because everything is in shambles or because other people live in our house.

A clean house exists for the good of people. The point is to keep our homes useful and functioning, not pristine. Our routines are how we execute that dance.

Routines Are Drills We Continue to Run

One mistake I've made more often than I can count is to start making up my routines with only a blank sheet of paper in front of me. I love to attempt a new set of routines from scratch.

However, these routines are doomed from the beginning because they're based on wishful thinking rather than reality. The best way to build routines is to connect them to the existing patterns of our day. By acknowledging our current reality we can slowly build up routines that fit our family's situation and needs.

How are you currently starting your day? When do you normally break for meals or transition to other activities? These are the moments we can harness, tying new and improved routines to these parts of our day.

It takes time and effort to implement a new routine, even when it is tied to an existing routine. Once established, however, the routine decreases the amount of time and effort needed to maintain it. That's the glory of routines.

A household run by routine isn't like a clock, never missing a beat and always exact. But routines do allow us to run a household with less mental, physical, and emotional effort. Making decisions at every juncture, for every need that arises, is exhausting and overwhelming. Routines remove the need to rehash every detail in our minds in order to decide what to do next.

Decision fatigue is real, and routines are the first line of defense for homemakers.

Decision fatigue is real, and routines are the first line of defense for homemakers. So much of the work we do will need to be done again that we might as well make it routine, regular, and repetitive, saving our decision-making energy for the situations that develop on the fly.

Just like you'd start a training program to become a runner, becoming an effective and cheerful home manager also requires a training program—one we never graduate from. Runners have to run to stay runners. Each individual runner determines how often and how long to run and what personal best record to work toward next. In the same way, our routines are a training program that we continue to modify and practice in order to stay in the game. Our abilities, our endurance, and our skills build up over time with routine practice.

Even a runner, however, doesn't follow the same program for the rest of his life. He has to deal with injuries. He sometimes needs to change things up in order to increase his speed, strength, or stamina. He might have a race on a new terrain that requires something different.

So it is for us at home. The same routines won't work after new babies, after a move, after illness, or during times of family upheaval. However, when we've practiced routines, we're able to come back to the game with an adapted version more quickly than if we had no routines at all. Don't try to shoehorn a new life into old routine structures; stretch and adapt your routines to fit your new circumstances.

Minimum Viable Routines

I don't know about you, but when I try to figure out a new set of routines, I generally try some rotation that ensures everything is covered. I want the best, most thorough, most complete routine ever. But those who want all or nothing generally get nothing, and it's no different with routines.

Instead of starting with the "best" plan, we should begin with the *minimum* plan that will make the most difference. We should ask ourselves, *What is the bare minimum needed to keep things running?* We can always build from there as we improve, and, just as importantly, we can return to the minimum viable option when (not if) life goes haywire.

Desiring a perfect routine turns out to be another cause of procrastination and resistance, because we all know we'll never execute the perfect routine. Sometimes the best way to overcome our resistance to a repetitive chore is to increase our repetitions, to practice it more—and we do that best when we start small.

For myself as well as hundreds of other women in our Convivial Circle community, three fifteen-minutes routines make all the difference long-term: a morning routine, an evening routine, and an EHAP routine. Let's develop each one.

Morning and Evening Routines

Mornings are critical to the success of a day, whether you're a morning person or not. With our mornings, we set the tone for ourselves and everyone else we're directing. We begin either by preparing and executing or by lounging and lazing. Very often, the way we begin is the way we carry out the rest of our day.

However, when we start our days with too much get-up-and-go, we risk crashing and burning by lunch. We don't want each day to be a repeated boom-and-bust cycle, with a morning boom and afternoon bust. We need a just-right-sized morning routine to establish momentum for the day. Similarly, the way we end one day shapes how we begin the next. We can collapse into bed, ignoring the fact that we'll have to be up to tackle the same struggles tomorrow, escaping into oblivion, or we can take a few minutes to set ourselves up for a strong start the next day. Just as the morning routine establishes the day's momentum, the evening routine is the gradual slow-down before the pit stop.

Morning and evening routines should be short and sweet, the bare minimum your household requires for just-get-by maintenance. Try selecting three tasks for the morning and three tasks for the evening that keep your home ready for action. These three tasks should take about fifteen minutes *total*—something that's manageable most days. These basic routines won't keep everything spic-and-span, but they will keep things running.

The EHAP Routine

EHAP is the midday routine. When I regularly carve out time for this routine in the afternoon, I can handle the intermittent chaos that attends the kids' work and play throughout the day. I know order will be restored, so I can take a deep breath and let them play without freaking out about the house.

We pronounce our afternoon tidy time, EHAP, as "ee-hap," like it's some sort of military maneuver. In a way, it is. I deploy my children, and we go on a seek-and-put-away mission. EHAP stands for Everything Has a Place. Of course, the implication is that everything should be *in* its place. It's family lingo for tidying up. If I ask them to EHAP, and then come in and see that not everything is in its place, then the room has not been EHAPed.

So it's a code word for returning anything out of place to its place, whether it be furniture, books, blankets, or toys. Nothing is exempt. Working together, we can usually have all the public areas of the house tidied up in fifteen minutes. Daily tidy-up rescue missions are the key to keeping the home ready for action.

With these three basic routines in place, we have traction. We have momentum. Added together, these three routines—morning, evening, and EHAP—take less than five hours a week, assuming we're taking one day off. Instead of barely keeping our heads above water, we start to see progress, even if we don't execute them completely and consistently every single day.

Routines Set—and Reset—the Stage

Our house is not a showpiece that matters simply because it exists. It is our husband, our children, and ourselves that matter because we exist, because we are made in God's image. Our house only matters because it is the stage that the drama of our lives is played upon. If the stage is impeding the action—either by being too messy or too clean—it's a problem.

> Our house only matters because it is the stage that the drama of our lives is played upon.

The props on our stage can be helpful or get in the way; they can help set the scene, or they can distract. So is it a clear setting? Or does clutter and grime interfere with the action?

Sometimes, it feels like dealing with the clutter and grime is an interruption to our "real lives," but that's wrong. The stage must be set and then reset, and that's our job. When we accept our role as stage manager, we're able to keep up a cheerful attitude in the midst of life's dramas.

What Is a Company-Ready Home?

As I've matured and gained more experience in friendship and hospitality, I've changed my definition of "company-ready." Being "company-ready" is less about the state of my house and more about the state of my heart.

Once, I was out running errands when my sister-in-law texted; she and her two small kids needed a place to kill an hour between other appointments. I wasn't home, but my kids were, and the cousins would have a good time together. It had been a big laundry day, and I had left the clean clothes half sorted on the couch.

I told them to stop by, and I refused to let myself feel embarrassed about being "caught" with laundry in the living room. It was mid-process, and it was out in the public space, but that's where I had space to make the piles I needed, and I was using my time as best I could—including being able to offer a pit stop for family.

By the time I got back home, my sister-in-law and her kids had already left. The laundry still sat there. I started dinner and kept going with the laundry. Remnants remained on the couch overnight, but I finished it up the next morning.

An impressive, visually calming organizational aesthetic is not what I have. Yet I like what I do have much better: a full life that is ready to be offered whenever needs and opportunities arise.

After all, my home is not a showcase for my style or my competence. It's just where we all live. Others are welcome to share that real life in process. Letting people into the middle of our lives fosters relationships and connection in a way that carefully styled dinner parties never can.

Letting people into the middle of our lives fosters relationships and connection in a way that carefully styled dinner parties never can.

Take a Baby Step to Start a Routine

Before dinner, call the kids and spend fifteen minutes—with a timer, all together—EHAPing: putting things away in their own home. Turn on music and make it a cheerful team effort. No matter how far you get, celebrate and be done when the timer goes off. Try it again tomorrow.

Where there are no oxen, the manger is clean, but abundant crops come by the strength of the ox.

—Proverbs 14:4

12

Step 6: Pursue Hospitality

Hospitality is living alongside others with generous conviviality

> Those who live out radically ordinary hospitality see their homes not as theirs at all but as God's gift to use for the furtherance of his kingdom.
>
> —Rosaria Butterfield, *The Gospel Comes with a Housekey*

When I was a teen, closing my bedroom door so Mom wouldn't see my mess was my primary "management" technique. I continued to use the technique as a young mother. When I had two small children and lived in a small rental, I did not stay on top of any of the cleaning in any room that wasn't public.

If I don't care and no one else sees it, then it's all OK, right?

One day, I invited an acquaintance to my home, an older mom who mentored me through a difficult loss. Just before she arrived, I discovered the water in the main bathroom wasn't working. The toilet would not flush.

There was another bathroom, but no time to get it ready. The house had hard water, and the orange stains covered more square footage than the white of the tile underneath. I hadn't cleaned it in I don't know how long—the weeks might have been measured in double digits. On top of that, you had to walk through my closet to get to this bathroom, and there were more clothes on the floor than there were hanging up.

My guest arrived, and I prayed she wouldn't have to use the bathroom.

An hour and a half later, just before she had to leave, she asked where the bathroom was. I apologized and said the toilet wasn't working. With genuine concern for us, she asked, "Is there another bathroom?" I had to admit there was. She said she really did need to use it and didn't care what state it was in. As I showed her the way, waves of mortification engulfed me.

That was probably the first time I was forced to admit that how we live and how we keep things—or don't—*does* matter. It turned out my friend needing to use that bathroom was God's answer to my prayer. It was the opposite of what I had requested, but it was exactly what I *needed*.

It was my wake-up call.

Suddenly, instead of living in my head and telling myself I didn't care that things weren't "perfect," I was forced to admit that I did care, at least a little. Maybe I needed to care a bit more than I did.

Your Kids Aren't Messing Up Your House

Homes are meant for hospitality. Hospitable homes are tools used in the formation of people, not trophies to be kept beautiful. Although our homes are not trophies, we also don't want them to be pigsties because we aren't raising pigs. As homemakers, we're making homes that shape the bodies and souls of humanity.

Although our homes are not trophies, we also don't want them to be pigsties because we aren't raising pigs.

Those souls' bodies might have been shaped in our wombs or not. Those bodies might sleep between sheets we wash or not. But our goal is that all the bodies and souls under our roof for years or for hours be shaped for good by the time spent in our homes.

If those people make a mess—a physical mess, an emotional mess, or any other kind of mess—it's not frustrating our goal or ruining our home. It's giving us the opportunity to use our home for its purpose: mending, serving, building.

Hospitality isn't something we do once the house is clean and we have our act together. Hospitality is loving others in and with our homes; love is the whole point.

Hospitality is building up people, and that's our mission, whether we started from the moment of their birth or we only just learned their name. With hospitality as a goal instead of a garnish and our homes as tools instead of trophies, we can see the evidence of people being built up in our homes as successes rather than frustrations.

One thing that makes hospitality difficult is that we tend to be out of practice. It's easy to slip into selfish patterns, doing what needs to be done on our own agendas, taking a break, keeping to ourselves and our own thoughts. Instead, we need to practice the habit of breaking out into hospitality.

The habit of hospitality includes but is much broader than having people over for dinner. It means inviting people into our lives—even the people who live in our houses. It is not enough to simply share a roof with people. We need to share a *life*—a full life, a conversational life—with them. Yes, it means more work, but that's what we're here for; the work is good.

A hospitable life will overflow into the lives of others through invitations and conversations, but mostly through our demeanor. The way we treat people is either selfish or welcoming, inviting, and interested. When we practice a convivial approach with our family, it will become how we treat others as well. The habit of hospitality will shape all our interactions.

> The habit of hospitality will shape all our interactions.

Have you ever had a waitress at a restaurant hover over your table, ready to pounce on your plate if you give the least indication that you're done? It's obnoxious, and it makes you feel like she'd prefer you to leave ASAP.

You probably leave a smaller tip, gripe a bit, and get out of her way. No one wants to stay where they feel unwelcome and unwanted. Yet how often are we like that pouncy waitress, tapping our toes, waiting for people to be done so we can clear their stuff? Clearing glasses left out because we want our counters clear, we then grumble about the number of glasses used per day.

We shouldn't be cleaning in order to maintain a lofty ideal of what our house should be like. Nor should we ignore our work for our own ease or convenience. We're taking care of people's real, physical needs, whatever the chore at hand. Let each of us look not only to our own interest, but also to the interests of others (Phil. 2:4).

Homes Are for Hospitality

Hospitality is not the same as entertaining. Entertaining is about impressing others and making ourselves look good; hospitality is about serving others and sharing life. The dictionary defines hospitality as "The quality or disposition of receiving and treating guests and strangers in a warm, friendly, generous way."

Warm. Friendly. Generous. Yes, that's right, part of the very definition of the word *hospitality* has to do not with your home, but with your attitude, your disposition, your heart. So we begin right at the core. Hospitality is not the same as entertaining guests, and it's not about showing off our homes.

Hospitality is a Christian duty and calling, and it is about showing love rather than demonstrating how put together we are. One too often overlooked aspect of hospitality is our attitude of hospitality—or is *hostility* closer to reality?—to our home's first guests: its residents.

Particularly when we are preparing to welcome dinner guests, it is all too easy to get short and snippy and frustrated with the children God has given to us as long-term guests. We prioritize our pride in our home (and our need for others' good opinions) over our own family. Tearing them down with our words or actions is not a good way to start off a day of hospitality.

If hospitality is building up the body of Christ, it must begin within our own families and then overflow to others. Otherwise, it is likely not true Christian hospitality but something we do so that others will think well of us. It is a cover for our insecurities rather than a genuine offering of ourselves to others.

Housework matters because our environment matters, the atmosphere our family grows in matters, and the ability to invite people into our homes matters. Housework is hospitality. It is hospitable care of oneself. It is hospitable care of one's family. It makes possible the hospitable care of others.

We often want to dismiss housework as trivial, not worth our valuable time (but perhaps worth someone else's time if we can pay them). Margaret Kim Peterson admonishes us in *Keeping House*, "Housekeeping is part of a tradition that takes seriously the basic, homely needs of people for food and clothing and shelter. These are needs that God takes seriously and that Jesus encourages Christians to take seriously."

Housekeeping is the most basic type of service—a foot-washing sort of service—that we often think is beneath us but that Jesus expressly commends. It is foolishness to the world, but it is a good work God calls us to walk in, a good work He blesses.

Offering Hospitality to Our Families First

Pursue hospitality. It's a command. It's a duty. But it doesn't mean we need to have people over for dinner every week. Well, except for *our* people—we feed them every week, every day—three times a day, even. That's hospitality, too.

A hospitable mindset means we see our home as a tool in the formation of people and homemaking as a process, a service of love to those who live in and enter into our home. Cleaning is an act of love.

I think few household chores are more loving than cleaning bathrooms. Cleaning a bathroom is pretty much the equivalent of changing diapers. There are unpleasant smells; there are bodily fluids; there are more of both not long after it's been cleaned. We understand that leaving a baby in his filth is unloving. It's our job to change the diaper, even if accidents happen in the midst of it.

Keeping bathrooms clean for our kids after they're potty-trained is the same kind of job. Not only does cleanliness in the privacy of a bathroom prevent the spread of germs, it also instills a sense of worth and dignity, even if they don't know it and we don't see it.

Do you want your kid to be grossed out by or comfortable in a disgusting bathroom? The bathroom he uses every day is shaping his expectations and tastes. This is alarming but true. Even if he goes off to a college dorm someday and never cleans his bathroom, you want him to know it's not good. That will only happen if he's been used to having a clean bathroom all his life.

Love is a sacrificial action more than it is a feeling. Feeling it without working it out in visible ways isn't real love. Cleaning house isn't merely a necessity we'd all abolish if we could. It's a true means of loving one another tangibly. Recognizing it as a means of love, we can come to love the work itself.

Maybe our kids or even our husband won't appreciate the behind-the-scenes work we do that "magically" makes bathrooms "stay" clean or causes clean clothes to appear in drawers, but that's part of the nature of blessing someone.

To give with grace is to give without looking for appreciation, fully satisfied in performing loving service regardless of receiving credit. Does God bestow favors on us that we don't appreciate and don't even notice? You bet. So we, too, can bestow some favors on others and say, "Thank you, Lord, for Your mercy" as we do.

> To give with grace is to give without looking for appreciation, fully satisfied in performing loving service regardless of receiving credit.

This doesn't mean we have to be the ones doing it all. But if we are, we need not be resentful. When they're old enough, it's even more gracious and merciful long-term to bring the kids along to help. Clean clothes are just as loving and magical if the kids help with the process—plus, they learn how to get clean clothes from dirty ones, which is valuable experience.

Knowing how to clean a bathroom is a useful skill to someone accustomed to clean bathrooms. A teen might think he'd rather use a dirty bathroom than scrub toilets, but that's just innate foolishness bound up in the heart of a child, and it's our job to drive it from them with repeated, enforced practice.

A Convivial Tone Is a Hospitable Tone

Hospitality to people outside our family gives us clues about offering hospitality to our own. We've already acknowledged that we switch to a different tone of voice when we answer the door or the phone. Why is that? It ought not be because we're presenting a fake self to others, but because we are being courteous and putting their needs above our own mood.

A family wherein each member looks to the interest of the others rather than trying to grab what he can is a welcoming, loving, joyful family. A happy family isn't one wherein each individual insists upon everyone else catering to him, but one where each person actively puts others' needs ahead of his own. It's the logic of the gospel, beautiful in practice though crazy-sounding to those without the gospel themselves.

Like it or not, moms set the tone of the home. After all, our children—for a significant portion of their lives—spend most of their waking hours with us. From us, they learn their communication patterns, their response habits, their work ethic. That's not to say they'll become carbon copies of us, of course. However, when God works to refine us, our children will also reap blessings from our sanctification.

The beauty of changing your tone to reflect what it ought to be rather than what comes naturally to you in the moment is that, when done in love without bitterness, we find our natural tone and mood are lifted as well. As Scripture says, "Whoever brings blessing will be enriched, and one who waters will himself be watered" (Prov. 11:25).

Hospitality both requires and produces growth; it takes time and practice. Love, empathy, and even conversational skills develop with cultivation. This is another way of saying hospitality takes work. But like all forms of discipline, it's worth it. It's about sharing life: its joys and sorrows, its embarrassments and its triumphs. Hospitality is living and loving genuinely together.

Too often, society's default understanding is that being authentic and "sharing life" means being discourteous and rude. "Being real" means letting our worst side show and expecting others to love us anyway, rather than loving them more than ourselves by fighting our selfish desires and putting their comfort and interests above our own.

Manners are love displayed in little things. What are some things we do for guests that can inform how we treat our family? How can we, as homemakers, make our home welcoming for those who live there? After all, isn't that the point of homemaking?

In what small ways can we make our love seen and felt throughout mundane days? Hospitality gives us clues.

Should we not also put forth the effort, the energy, the self-discipline to love those within our home with our eyes, our mouths, our expressions, and our tones? Think about that switch that flips when you answer the phone, and pray for the strength to flip that switch for the sake of each person within your home.

Someday They Will Be Guests

I remember when my husband began working remotely from home. It was 2012, almost a decade before most of the rest of the world got a chance to try it out. Because it was a typical homeschool day, one of the kids was in math tears. I was not handling it well, but I didn't notice. My mind was preoccupied with all I'd hoped to do today, but instead I was stuck with a math drama llama.

I hadn't even noticed that I'd started to raise my voice. I didn't notice the edge in my tone or the sharpness of my words. Yet there I was, about to hit the limit on my patience-o-meter and really lose my cool when my husband walked up the stairs to refill his water, paused, and asked, "Something wrong?"

Stopped in my tracks, suddenly I saw the situation from a third-party view rather than from my preoccupied stance. Something *was* wrong, and it was me who was causing the problem. I changed my tone, and we were able to tackle the math problem.

Although I'm nowhere near perfect, ever since that day I've been more self-conscious about the way I speak to the kids. How would I speak to a friend who was having a similar issue? How would I treat a guest sitting down to dinner?

I am so grateful God brought my tone to my attention when He did, because now that two of my children *are* adult guests in my home when they're around, I realize that my manners helped me make the transition to relating to them as responsible adults. I'm no longer pretending to treat them as friends, but they *are* friends and co-laborers in the Lord, not my wards or chess pieces for me to maneuver.

Take a Baby Step to Offer Hospitality

Remember that the child you're upset with today will be an adult guest in your home before you know it. The way you relate now is laying the groundwork for your relationship then. Ask your child's forgiveness whenever you sin against him.

Show hospitality to one another without grumbling.

—1 Peter 4:9

PART 3

Loving a Homemaker's Life

Christ, whose glory fills the skies,
Christ the true, the only Light,
Sun of Righteousness, arise,
Triumph o'er the shades of night;
Dayspring from on high, be near;
Daystar in my heart appear.

Dark and cheerless is the morn
Unaccompanied by Thee;
Joyless is the day's return
Till Thy mercy's beams I see;
Till they inward light impart,
Glad my eyes, and warm my heart.

Visit then this soul of mine;
Pierce the gloom of sin and grief;
Fill me, Radiancy divine,
Scatter all my unbelief;
More and more Thyself display,
Shining to the perfect day.

—Charles Wesley (1707–1788)

13

Organization Is Like Laundry

We can rejoice in the repetition of life

A child kicks his legs rhythmically through excess, not absence, of life. Because children have abounding vitality, because they are in spirit fierce and free, therefore they want things repeated and unchanged. They often say, "Do it again"; and the grown up person does it again till he is nearly dead. For grown up people are not strong enough to exult in monotony. But perhaps, God is strong enough to exult in monotony. It is possible that God says every morning, "Do it again" to the sun; and every evening, "Do it again" to the moon.

—G. K. Chesterton, *Orthodoxy*

I used to avoid folding the laundry because it bothered me that I'd just have to do it again. It wouldn't stay done, so why do it at all? Whether or not the laundry is folded hasn't always been a reliable indicator of faithfulness in my life. As a barometer, it would give false readings.

There have certainly been times when the clean laundry lived in baskets because I was too apathetic to put it away. Laundry baskets are functional drawers, aren't they?

But there have been times when the laundry baskets were empty because the hampers were festering, when the washer had to run multiple times because I was too lethargic or distracted to get the damp clothes into the dryer.

Some days the kitchen laundry went straight into the drawer, unfolded, not because I didn't care, but because I decided it was fine for the infant to play with the contents of that drawer while I made dinner and did dishes.

There was the season in a smallish rental without any drawers or dressers, and my husband decided a laundry basket in the closet piled with clean whites counted as his drawer. For several years before that, I'd sorted his things into his drawers most of the time.

Before that, in the season of babies, toddlers, and teaching kids to read and use the bathroom, my husband declared that just getting clean clothes in baskets into our bedroom was perfectly adequate, and I was to spend my time doing more important things than folding laundry.

In sum, the location of the clean laundry has never been a reliable indicator of how I'm doing with my duties. Some years, laundry in the baskets meant negligence. Others, it meant obedience and aligned priorities. This is as it ought to be. The laundry itself was never the end, just a means.

The Problem Isn't Repetition

A great source of our frustration, despondency, and fussiness about life at home is due to unrealistic expectations—false ideas about what it's "supposed" to be like. We usually think about life's successes in terms of accomplishments, things that are done and done well.

Housework is not the kind of thing that is ever really "done" in this sense. Wanting the laundry to be done once and for all is to want laundry to be something other than what it is. By its very nature, laundry must be done regularly, over and over. If we're working hard with the goal of "finishing" it, then there is no hope. We can only be frustrated because laundry will always return, and rather quickly.

Instead, laundry—and all the other chores, too—must be one of those things we just keep plugging away at. Sometimes there is more, sometimes there is less, sometimes we're keeping up, and sometimes we aren't. After we aren't, it takes extra time to do some extra loads until we get our groove and our laundry generation rate aligned again.

Nor does the same laundry plan work in perpetuity. The routines and habits that worked in the newly married state are not the same as those that work in the newborn state which are not the same as those that work in the passel-of-children state. Perhaps there is farm dirt. Perhaps there are oil and mechanical grime. Perhaps there are many collared shirts to iron. The laundry to be done reflects and supports the rest of our lives. Like our lives, laundry requires change.

Like our lives, laundry requires change.

Through laundry, we can understand life better, can understand the nature of all the rest of our work at home for our families and for the maintenance of family life. Those jeans come again through the laundry pile not because something is wrong or because you didn't clean them well enough before, but because life rolls ever on. The work to be done was done, and now it's time to do it again.

The same is true with dishes. The dirty plates and pots reflect a family that eats: a mundane, happy truth. There is no home routine magic that will make the dishes done once and for all. If that's the goal, then it would be best to stop eating.

The same is true of dirty floors, dust on the shelves, fingerprints on the windows, clutter on the counters. Too often, we look for solutions that will make the work go away when what we actually need are solutions that will keep us consistently, repetitively doing the work needed.

Just like the goal of the laundry is not to have it completed, so the goal of any housekeeping job is not for it to be completed. Laundry, dishes, and dusting teach us about life itself. Life is full of ongoing work that we continue to do because it continues to accrue.

As we continually do the repetitive work of our home, we can learn that we also must continually do the work of our heart, which won't be static and stay clean until Jesus returns. The outside work mirrors the inside work and vice versa. In both, we can plug away daily in ten-minute chunks, content with faithful plodding.

Persist in Patient Practice

The fact that housework won't be done in this life does not need to discourage us. Instead, we can choose to practice, to make progress, and to give up on our false hopes of being "done." The room doesn't have to stay clean for it to be worth your time to clean it.

As I drove home after dropping off the older kids at swim team one day, I thought about how good it was for them to have to get up and go do something they didn't feel like doing in the moment because they had committed to it. They might grumble as they get in the car, but in the end, they like it. When I got home, it hit me: If that's a good thing, then it's good for me, too. According to my plan, that day was supposed to be a run day, but I didn't want to. I did want the fruit of having run—the extra energy, the stronger muscles, the baby weight gone—but I didn't want to *practice* the running.

The room doesn't have to stay clean for it to be worth your time to clean it.

It's so annoying when parenting applies to us. It generally turns out that we need character training just as much (or more) than our kids. It is good for us to get up—not only in the morning but at any point during the day—and practice something worthwhile, even if we don't feel like it in the moment.

We need patience not only when we are tempted to anger and frustration, but also for the work that pays off later. We need patience wrapped up in fortitude, in forgoing instant gratification in exchange for the long-term reward. Patience is a part of perseverance, and it is grown by practicing it, by doing the work that is less pleasant at the time but will later yield abundance.

When we get the hang of that perspective shift, we're not going to be at the finish line. We keep learning and growing without looking for an endpoint version of success. Success is learning and growing, walking faithfully, every day.

Success is not fulfilling all our duties perfectly. It *is* that, through our duties, we walk in repentance and faithfulness and love with God. Just as the goal of the laundry is not to have all the laundry complete, so the goal of any other housekeeping job is not for it to be complete.

> Success is learning and growing, walking faithfully, every day.

Sure, learning and growing is a good thing, and practice does increase our skills, but we can't postpone doing our duties until we've reached an imaginary state where we feel ready and pulled together. That state feels like a moving, unachievable target because it *is*, not because we're doing it wrong.

Living a Laundry-Driven Life

True confession: I've tried every laundry routine out there and never found one that enabled me to stay on top of the laundry. I can discover a good rhythm, but then something will change. I finally realized that one factor is that laundry is not evenly produced over time. In winter, the clothes are bulkier, so fewer fit of them in the washing machine, meaning there are more loads to do. In summer, swimsuits and towels regularly need quick rinses and a dry cycle.

Little kids have little clothes, but they get them dirty at a fast and furious rate. The amount of laundry varies with activities, weather, and health (or lack thereof). If by a "consistent" laundry routine, I meant I was looking to do the same work and get the same result day in and day out, then I was dooming myself to failure with false expectations.

Big kids have big clothes, and big kids can learn to do some laundry. But big kids have their own ideas about how they're going to spend their time, and it doesn't usually fit with my desire to have the load out of the laundry room.

People get sick. Illness becomes a compound problem because it generates more laundry and takes the laundress or her minions (or both) out of commission. Extra laundry is heaped up and becomes a backlog.

Life gets busy. The rhythm, for a day or two or even a week, becomes untenable. Routines are dropped for the sake of a family emergency, extra hospitality, or big life events. Sometimes routines are suspended simply because the needs of everyday life have added up and require all our attention and time. The laundry is forgotten, and forgotten laundry quickly becomes Mt. Washmore, looming before us in overwhelming heaps.

Instead of pronouncing ourselves laundry failures when there is a lot of laundry to do, we need to shift our perspective and approach. Not only will the laundry never be finished (and remember, it's not supposed to be), it also fluctuates dramatically. Our job as homemakers is not to figure out automations (that is, plans or systems or routines) that generate equal results, day after day and week after week. Instead, our job is to live responsively, dancing the dance of home life.

It's the same with being organized. Sometimes life chugs along at a fairly even keel. We develop patterns that work and keep things consistent. We might be tempted to call that—and only that—a time we are "organized." If that's what organized looks like, we assume we have to have a certain set of circumstances to be organized. The reality, however, is that being organized is about how we handle life, not about what kind of life we're in.

Being organized is about how we handle life, not about what kind of life we're in.

Sometimes life is wildly variable and unpredictable. Sometimes we're in crisis mode. When we're organized—in our attitude and approach—we can ride the waves.

When we call other people "organized," we usually mean they seem like they have their act together. We imagine they must be the kind of person whose closets stay tidy and whose fridge never sees spills. Basically, we conjure up a picture of the person we would like to be, then project it onto someone else. Perhaps it's a way to clutch at the hope that our ideals *are* possible.

I would say I'm organized, but that's not because my house is always clean. My house is always a launching pad of action. Something is always happening, so there's endless flux. Being organized means being able to handle flux and activity without freaking out. Now that I'm organized, I know what to do when things are wildly out of hand, and I dedicate the time to rein it all back in as needed.

Recently, I was sick. I had a sinus headache, my ears hurt, and I slept in the middle of the afternoon even after drinking some coffee. There was no A game to bring to the day for multiple days on end—but everyone else was still going full-bore. I couldn't ask them to pick up my slack. Clutter piled up. The counters were grimy. Laundry collected in baskets.

The house and family still functioned. It was temporary, and we could all handle things being subpar. The wise call was to let everyone else keep doing their thing and catch up with the maintenance when I got better, not make everyone else redirect their energies so that the house could stay clean.

I did get better. Then I spent two hours whipping things back into shape with some help from the kids, and no one and nothing was the worse for the wear. Houses can be readily cleaned up. Stuff can be put away. Being organized is being able to handle that work without damaging relationships and without declining into needless inner turmoil about it.

I am organized because I'm not afraid to roll up my sleeves and do what needs to be done to keep things rolling. While I was sick, that meant sleeping instead of cleaning or worrying. After I was better, I jumped back in the game.

Lorra's Baby Steps to Rejoice in Repetition

When Lorra Wells joined the Convivial Circle community, she felt like she was failing at homemaking. She was frustrated because of all the stuff in her house and her seemingly endless piles of laundry. Resenting the amount of time it took her to keep house, she found it difficult to make herself follow through on her plans.

Although skeptical at first, she tried a brain dump and an alignment card, both of which helped her notice her thought patterns. Working through the Simplified Organization courses[1], she realized that all the tasks on her list were simply ways to love God and love people. Her attitude and her priorities then began to shift. Instead of seeing the laundry as an endless pile she was supposed to conquer, she began thinking of it as a way to bless her family and allow them to be more serviceable in their day.

Before, each task on her list was something she was supposed to make go away. As she practiced not only better basic routines but better stories about her routines, her interpretation of her tasks changed. She was able to count herself successful, even if all the tasks weren't checked off.

---

1 See Appendix A.

She found that a daily card and weekly review were the keys to getting the right things done. Giving up a desire for a silver bullet that would help her master all her work, she began to iterate and work on shorter-term interval plans instead of grand schemes. As she did, she developed motivation and commitment to keep making small improvements.

In the end, it wasn't that the nature or amount of work changed, but that Lorra changed. She started with her attitude about the work, she started doing the work before she felt like she had it figured out, and by relating to it rightly, she ended her discouragement. More than that, without ever "conquering" her list or her chores, she became able to appreciate that each small step was meaningful. Each repetition mattered, so she could choose each one with joy.

> *Moreover, it is required of stewards that they be found faithful.*
>
> —1 Corinthians 4:2

14

Home Is Where the Happiness Is

Fulfillment and satisfaction are the reward of meaningful work

> As Dr. Johnson said, "To be happy at home is the end of all human endeavour". (1st to be happy, to prepare for being happy in our own real Home hereafter: 2nd, in the meantime, to be happy in our houses.) We wage war in order to have peace, we work in order to have leisure, we produce food in order to eat it. So your job is the one for which all others exist.
>
> —C. S. Lewis in a letter to Mrs. Johnson

After thirty years of living in a messy bedroom, I did not feel at home in a tidy space. I didn't want to call myself a messy person—but it was true. After all, I was uncomfortable when my own bedroom was neat and clean. It just didn't seem like my room.

When I finally realized that clean rooms caused me discomfort, I resigned myself to long-haul change. My problem was bigger and deeper than could be fixed by a weekend cleaning spree. Sure, I needed the cleaning blitz, but that was not the only thing I needed.

I also needed time to acclimate. Gradual change is easier to grow accustomed to than an abrupt overhaul. I selected small sections of my bedroom at a time and focused on keeping them tidy. When messes overtook me again, I started my efforts with those previously reclaimed areas.

I needed to push back against the discomfort. My resistance was not a signal that something was wrong, but that I was growing. I was experiencing growing pains, which I could ignore because good inner work was happening beneath them.

In order to become a person who lives in and prefers order and cleanliness, I had to actually notice it. After cleaning, I began to pause and survey rather than move on to the next thing. Every time I looked around my room, I would notice what was neat and think affectionate thoughts about that area. I would also notice the untidy places (like my closet floor) and add them to my Saturday to-do list not with guilt, but with the assumption that I would prefer my shoes in paired, straight lines.

A tidy bedroom was—and continues to be—a work in progress for me. But after taking the time to pause and notice what was good and what was bad, I felt the shift. I started picking things up automatically rather than out of guilt or a feeling of obligation. I was *happy* when the house was clean. I enjoyed walking through my room in the dark and knowing I wouldn't trip. Traction happened slowly, picking up speed and momentum the longer I gave it scraps of my attention amidst the other details of life.

Families Need Homes

Not only does Scripture say much about the family, it also uses families as a metaphor for our relationship with God. How can we understand, much less embody, the truths given in Scripture unless we're invested in our own families? "God sets the lonely in families," proclaims Psalm 68:6 (NIV), which means we need to be families ready for the hospitality God has prepared for us to offer.

> The family as a tool of blessing–of privilege, even–is no accident. It is the way God structured the world.

The family as a tool of blessing—of privilege, even—is no accident. It is the way God structured the world. Those who tear apart families—who deny the necessity and value of families, who hate and envy the privilege others have due to intact families—are tearing society apart. The effects can be clearly seen by anyone willing to notice. Society needs strong, intelligent women who invest themselves with energy and industry in homes and families, no matter what slanders the world levels at us.

A functioning Christian family is so fundamental to God's plan that one half of a married couple is devoted to cultivating it with all her creative and productive energy. The other half is then charged with providing for it and protecting it. According to Ephesians 5, a wife is the picture of the church, a living proclamation of the fruitfulness and beauty of the gospel.

The home is more than a place to refuel with food and sleep. The home is the hub for humanity. Within the home, people have responsibilities to one another, relationships are knit together, and communities are formed.

The home is more than a place to refuel with food and sleep. The home is the hub for humanity.

The world is dark, without question. Perhaps the news makes you want to hunker down and hide in your home. Home is exactly where we need to turn, but not in order to hunker or hide.

Home is where the troop reinforcements are found and from whence they are deployed. Home is where society begins, so women are the backbone of society. Home is a refuge from the world, but not merely a refuge. Home is base. Without a base, the army can't deploy.

If society is falling apart, it is because homes fell apart first. Society is not a replacement for families. Societies do not run in parallel with families. Societies are *made* of families. And families are made in homes.

From the beginning, humans were created to live in community. It was not good for man to be alone; alone, a man could not fulfill his mission. People are made in God's image, and one way we reflect our triune God is by being individuals living in social harmony. The family is a society more fundamental than that of the nation or the church, for it must exist if the others are to exist.

Let us focus our whole selves on the gospel work of building families, homes, and communities. If we focus our efforts on building up healthy, happy people, the world will feel the impact—even if it never knows why it happened or where the change began.

Homes Foster Happiness

Happiness is a function of having right relationships, not of having material ease or comfort or affluence. When we are living in properly ordered, loving relationships, we will be satisfied and happy. Of course, the most important relationship is with our Creator, Savior, and Lord. When we are in fellowship with God, His mercy and forgiveness flow out of us and bind us to those God has given us: our husband, our children, our church, our society.

Housework, with all its ups and downs and overflows, reflects rhythms of real life. As we learn to adapt, expanding and contracting our time with the work as needed, we are learning how to handle a people-oriented rather than a project-oriented life. Relationships are messy. Relationships take unschedulable maintenance; relationships are also a primary source of happiness.

Women function as relational glue. Therefore, we will be satisfied and joyful the more we embrace and the better we employ this role. Men can't have family without women; we bind fathers to their children. Women have always been the social force connecting communities—made obvious in the difference between the American colonists who came as families and those who came as marauding conquerors.

The classical concept of happiness saw it as a fruit of virtue, of excellence. When we live rightly, fulfilling the design and mission we were created for, we will be happy. The hedonists are wrong: we were not created for material pleasure. Therefore, ease and affluence will not bring happiness. The Marxists are wrong: we are not the sum of our economic contribution or our political power. Having more power or more money will not make us happy.

Christianity, on the other hand, is true: we are created to glorify God and enjoy Him forever. We enjoy God when we function where He puts us and how He commands us. God's commands aren't given as some mere test of will, but to tell us how to rightly relate to Him and the world He made. When we love God and walk obediently in faith, we are blessed, and we are happy.

> When we love God and walk obediently in faith, we are blessed, and we are happy.

I don't become happy by putting myself first, whether that's by prioritizing my own pleasure, my ease and convenience, or my desires. None of these brings happiness in its wake. Happiness is a by-product of living in accordance with our created purpose. The more we ignore or actively fight that purpose, the more unhappy we will be.

In contrast, the more we embrace and embody our creational nature—our design to be active, productive worshippers of the triune God—the happier we will be, because we are being what we were created to be. In heaven, we will be forever satisfied and happy, not because we'll be effortlessly floating on clouds, but because we'll be constantly in fellowship with God.

As God's redeemed people, we can begin partaking of that joy now. When we do, we realize the truth of Nehemiah 8:10: "The joy of the Lord is your strength." We need strength to walk by faith. We need strength to be zealous for good works as God commands.

Thus, we need joy, which is a fruit of the Holy Spirit abiding in us; we have access to joy because we have the Spirit. Our joy, our happiness, is not dependent on our circumstances because our happiness comes straight from the indwelling Spirit. As long as we are abiding in Christ, we have joy and strength.

Homemakers Need a Dose of Good Humor

It's easy to get down, to be negative, to critique everything, to become wrapped up in getting things done. Unfortunately, when we are absorbed in our lists and ourselves, we often see others as interruptions. We make the atmosphere of our home worse, not better, even as we think we're trying hard.

We do need to work hard. Hard work isn't the problem. The problem is that we take ourselves too seriously. We need to be able to dig into our work with good humor. When we laugh in the midst of our busy day, we remember that being human is about more than getting things done.

When we laugh with our kids, we build our relationship with them. Laughter brings us out of our self-centeredness and gives us perspective. Smiles, jokes, and laughter build the home atmosphere we want far faster and far better than vacuumed floors and dusted baseboards.

When we get so frustrated and irritated and single-minded that we can't smile at our children and be amused by their foibles, we're probably falling into the trap of self-importance. Self-reliance, self-importance, and self-righteousness are the fastest roads to burnout. The solution is to laugh the laugh of joy, of faith, of hope.

If you can't laugh when your children act like children, it's a sign you need to dig deep and get help from your husband or friends to climb out of your critical mental rut. Simply looking for and laughing at the funny side of life is one way out of burnout, fatigue, and overwhelm.

It's easy to slip into correction mode and stay there all the time, being negative and critical as a habit—critical of our husbands, our kids, and ourselves. We need to find ways to break the habit of negativity, whether that's with jokes or spontaneous dance parties to a fun playlist.

When you feel tense and uptight, step back and observe the situation. If this situation was on a TV show, everyone would be laughing at it, right? So I could take a step back and pretend I'm the audience, not in the middle of it, and say, "OK, this is actually kind of funny."

Remember Proverbs 31:25: "She laughs at the time to come." The Proverbs 31 woman's laughter comes from more than a sense of humor. Her ability to take the days in stride without frustration and anxiety comes from her trust in God and confidence in His care. The weight of the world, the burden of how our children turn out, the reality of entropy do not need to lie heavy on our shoulders. Jesus carries us. He cares more than we do, and He is bringing about His glory in the world. We can rest in Him.

Proclaiming the Gospel in Living Metaphor

When my husband wraps up his workday and emerges from his office, I like to be in the kitchen making dinner or standing at a table or the bed folding laundry. When I was a young wife, I was advised to tidy up the house and myself before my husband came home from work. My implementation was quite spotty, but it was only in implementation that I began to understand the wisdom.

After several years, I began to see that it was good advice, not because I needed to prove I had done something or because I should put on a show for the good of my husband, but because our coming together—in every way, at any time—was the heart of our family, of our home. It was worth preparing for. The husband-and-wife meeting is the key moment of dramatic tension and meaning enacted daily.

If we come into each other's company without regard for one another, we are not telling the truth about Jesus and His bride. If we're each wrapped up in our own projects and our own separate lives, we're living like roommates rather than like husband and wife. As the heart of the home, the attractive center of the home, I set the tone for our relationship and for our family life by how I greet my husband.

When my husband started working from home, the pulse of the home changed. The afternoon tidy-up was no longer a preparation of the home for Dad to return, because Dad was there all day, seeing a stop-motion picture of our home life with each trip to the bathroom or kitchen. But the point was never to pretend life hadn't been lived while he was away at work. The point was always to give attention to the way we came together.

With my husband working from home, we meet and greet many, many times throughout the day. Even so, we are not to live like roommates nor like coworkers, passing in the hall, absorbed with our own selves. In the midst of a busy day full of good, productive, fruitful work, we are husband and wife. We kiss when we meet.

How we relate as husband and wife is designed to be a pictured proclamation of the gospel. Every marriage is either truthful or lying about Jesus and His body, His bride, the church. There will be no marriage in heaven because we will have the fullness, the completion of being with Christ. We won't need the pictures marriage and family offer us anymore. For now, however, we have the privilege and responsibility of living out a microcosm of the gospel.

The world needs more gospel in it, and every functioning Christian family is a mini gospel message, shining light into the dark world. Ephesians 5 teaches us that marriage proclaims the gospel, and it explains how it does so. "Wives, submit to your own husbands, as to the Lord" (v. 22).

The world needs more gospel in it, and every functioning Christian family is a mini gospel message, shining light into the dark world.

If we are fulfilling our part of the picture of the gospel that marriage was designed to proclaim, portraying the glory and beauty of the church, the body of Christ, then we are the very aroma of God's work in the world. What would the world be without a faithful church? It would be as barren and marauding as a band of missionless men without wives and children.

The husband loves his wife sacrificially, as Jesus gave Himself for His bride. Having given Himself, Jesus then gave His bride a mandate to be fruitful. That's what brides do: They receive and they glorify. They take raw resources and transform them into productive beauty—marital love into children, paychecks into hot meals on the table, land into flowers and tomatoes, houses into homes.

Happiness at home isn't found by achieving a trendy aesthetic, by defining a personal style, or by arranging everything for our own convenience. Instead, happiness is found when we live the metaphor we were given. It's a full, interesting, meaningful mission in the world that brings satisfaction and joy in its wake.

Rachel's Baby Steps to Happiness at Home

Rachel Aytes enrolled in Convivial Circle[2] just before making an international move to Thailand with her husband and four daughters. With so much to do, she didn't know how to prioritize or choose wisely in the moment. She wanted to feel confident that she was doing what was most important, but instead, she usually felt scattered and weary.

Although she was good at keeping her routines, she battled perfectionism and tended to assume that a total life overhaul would be the fix for feeling like she had too much to do and never enough time to do it. She was willing to set aside time to focus on her homemaking, and her persistence in working on her skills paid off once she realized half her problem was her own attitude.

Instead of perpetually seeking the just-right system, she began focusing on just doing the next right thing in front of her. At first, she resisted doing the daily card because it seemed too simplistic. She also didn't want to make a new one every day. However, she gave it a shot and found it helped her notice where she really was and what people needed from her each day.

She recognized that she resented her family needing things from her when she already had so much to do, so she

2 See Appendix A.

began giving thanks for interruptions and changes. Gradually, grace and joy replaced her grumbling and resentment. With her daily card of three tasks, she ended the day glad that her priorities had been accomplished whereas, before, she had often stared sadly at her still-too-long list.

Rachel applied this concept to her interval plan as well and forced herself to keep it to a half page. Keeping the space limited reminded her that *she* was limited. Her job was not to do all the things she could identify as needing doing, but to determine which ones mattered most right then. Practicing small changes and iteration gave her clarity, focus, and renewed enthusiasm.

Rachel's challenges in mothering and educating her kids haven't diminished. If anything, they've intensified. But she sees how God has used these challenges as a prompt to fix her eyes on Him so that she can run with endurance. She felt a real shift in her attitude, which gave her a renewed energy for the next season of life.

When things didn't go as planned, Rachel started praying with thanksgiving to refocus on what faithfulness really means. She realized it's not about checking things off her list, but about obeying God no matter what happens. "I am so thankful," she said, "My attitude has improved. I've seen growth in taming my inner two-year-old, who wants to pout when she doesn't get her way. That has freed me to focus on how I can be faithful in whatever circumstances may come my way."

Her recommendation for others is to just get started. Once she gave the daily card a consistent effort, she was surprised at how quickly her mood and productivity improved. It wasn't really the daily card, though; it was the fact that she was writing out her card with gratitude and an open hand. Because of her focus on serving Christ rather than finishing her list, she became flexible and confident, just as she had hoped.

> *And let our people learn to devote themselves to good works, so as to help cases of urgent need, and not be unfruitful.*
>
> —Titus 3:14

15

Balance Is an Illusion

Balance is not static equilibrium, but an active wobbling

All art involves conscious discipline . . . One is always having to neglect one thing in order to give precedence to something else. The question is one of priorities.

—Edith Schaeffer, *The Hidden Art of Homemaking*

It was almost April, and I had the itch to spring clean. I started with the pantry, pulling everything out, wiping down shelves, clearing out junk, and putting everything back in an orderly fashion. I even labeled the bins and containers so that my team of helpers could see where things go.

Then it was mid-May. We were wrapping up our school year, limping to the end. The list of things I'd tackle after we were done grew hour by hour. I eyed the pantry. It definitely went on the list.

Brown sugar had spilled at some point—not just onto the floor, but into other containers. What had been an orderly bin of reusable containers was a chaotic heap with many lids on the floor rather than in the stack. None of the bottles seemed to fit the bins, even though they all had only a few weeks before.

Someone had put a can of tomatoes in the bin labeled "Soup." Packages of pasta lay on the shelf, taking up too much room, even though there was a bin with plenty of room two feet away labeled "Pasta." Many items were inexplicably sticky.

What had happened?

Earlier in motherhood, I would have sighed in frustration and called the previous pantry organization a waste of time because it didn't last. I would have strategized new ways to organize and different ways to train my helpers so that my work wouldn't be undone.

Now, I was forty. One son had moved out and another was making preparations to do so. I knew it was more important that my children were competent and independent in the kitchen than that my pantry stayed neat and orderly—and one would preclude the other. I knew it was better that they did the dishes than that everything was put exactly where I wanted it.

> Messes don't indicate a problem to solve but simply where attention is needed next.

The messy pantry was just another item added to the list, again. No recrimination required. No failure felt. Such was simply the maintenance required by an active household raising capable children. Messes don't indicate a problem to solve but simply where attention is needed next.

True Balance Is Wobbly

When we say we want "balance," we tend to picture mechanical scales calibrated just so. We're looking for the proper proportions to keep things static.

True balance is not a matter of perfection, achievement, or equality. It is about making the needed adjustments as you go. True consistency is about continuously choosing the appropriate response, not doing the same thing no matter what.

Watch a ballerina balance. Watch a tight-rope walker consistently make it across the wire. Try yourself to balance on one foot. Successful human balance is neither frozen nor motionless. As you balance, you make tiny compensations throughout your whole body. If you start to topple, you can stay upright by moving back a bit. Even if you appear still from a distance, you can feel the tiny twitches within your body as you compensate for internal and external pressures.

It is the same in life. We are not seeking a frozen, perfected balance as if our life is a set of scales. We are in a human balancing act much more like a ballerina, who has strengthened her muscles enough to hold a position or change as needed, but whose body is always making micro-corrections.

The more we practice our core responses, the stronger they get and the easier they become. The stronger we get, the more we make it look effortless or even static. Yet we will always know, we will always feel, the tiny compensations being made as we go. Our balance is always a wobble, and this is as it should be.

We can have balance because we are not our own source of stability. God is our rock, and our stability is found in Christ. No matter how much we wobble, visibly or not, we can have a fundamental assurance, trust, and security—not in our ability to handle all things, but in God's ability to handle all things.

No life system or organizational method will eliminate struggle. We will always face times of derailment. That's life. It's not a problem with our habits or systems or us.

We will get derailed. The question is, will we get back up again? If we recover after a fall, we're faithfully keeping the balance. Don't use finding balance as a code for perfectionism. It's an easy trap to fall into, but perfectionism paralyzes. It steals our joy and undermines our true progress. Balance isn't a static state. It's perpetual adjusting.

> We will get derailed. The question is, will we get back up again?

Therefore, we can hold our plans loosely. A key part of wobbling in balance is to not grip our methods or plans too firmly, to not think that organizing means controlling anything other than ourselves. To be effective at home, with active families and busy lives, we have to be ready and willing to adjust. Time spent planning isn't time deciding how the future will unfold. Planning is simply preparing ourselves to handle what comes.

When we plan with our ultimate goal in mind—building up people—we're able to wisely and effectively adjust to the unexpected. We're able to wobble in balance.

Balance Takes Entropy into Account

We've all experienced entropy. It's a law of nature: if left to itself, everything tends toward disorder. Right after we've folded the towels, an infant crawls over them, spreading them around the room. We clean all the way to the corners in one area, only to find that the area we cleaned yesterday has been—heaven forbid—dirtied already. The grocery run we *just* made (or was it last week?) has been entirely consumed, and people are still hungry.

Entropy gets us every time. When God cursed the ground, He set entropy into motion. Gardens grow weeds, but so do homes, relationships, plans, and systems. The weeds look different depending on where we're looking, but the fact remains: the world tends toward disorder when left untended. This means tending—maintenance, continual effort—is the name of the game.

We've already talked about how the work of a home, by its very nature, is repetitive. We never clean the bathroom once and for all. We never catch up on the laundry once and for all. We never organize the closet once and for all.

Something will always happen to disrupt and confuse, one way or another, eventually. It will need to be redone. We can't tell ourselves it won't be. This is entropy.

We must tell ourselves the truth and make it a good story. We're organizing for fun. We're catching up on the laundry to kick off a new routine that will work better. We're cleaning the bathroom for guests. Next time we need to, we'll do it again.

If we want to handle life well, we have to take entropy into account in our mindset and our approach. We can choose a better attitude about entropy if we think of our housework and mothering as tending rather than Getting Things Done™. When we check things off, we want them to stay done, but our work at home is different. It is tending, caring, stewarding work, not project work.

We tend our home and our family when we care for the little needs, over and over. Tending with tenderness, we pull weeds—literally and metaphorically. Those weeds will come back, but we pull them when we see them. That is caring for our little spot.

When we care with affection for little things, our heart is more and more attached to them, and we fight the work less.

We'll discover that what we tend, we start tending *towards*. When we care with affection for little things, our heart is more and more attached to them, and we fight the work less. It takes time for such tendencies to form, but form they do.

Proper Balance Makes Us Steadfast

The dictionary defines the verb *balance* as "to keep or put something in a steady position so that it does not fall" or "to offset or compare the value of one thing with another."

The first definition is the one we usually mean when we talk about achieving balance in our lives. We want to be steady, regular, diligent, consistent. We hate feeling like we're scrambling, dropping the ball, and never getting to what matters, so we think balance is the answer.

But what is that *something* we're putting in a steady position so it doesn't fall? Is it our to-do list? Is it our various roles and responsibilities? Is it our attitude? Or is it all of the above?

In seeking the first definition of balance, we often settle for the second, which means we make trade-offs and hope everything will come out even in the end. We didn't get to the laundry, but the schoolwork was done. We didn't mop, but we did get dinner on the table. Does the value of what was done make up for what wasn't?

Sure, we want *all* the things done so that we never have to make trade-offs, but it's just not going to happen. We can continue honing our skills and getting better at what we do. We can expand our capacity and align our expectations. But we will always make trade-offs. We just need to make sure those trade-offs are done in favor of the work with ultimate value: cultivating hearts and relationships.

If we're going to keep anything in a steady position so it doesn't fall, let's make it our attitude, not our chores.

Keeping an even keel emotionally will keep the scales balanced, no matter what suffered in the day's survival-mode skirmish. Having a balanced emotional life is the best kind of balanced life to live.

After all, an even temper, a cheerful attitude, and a resilient and impervious demeanor protect what is of ultimate value. If our heart and relationships aren't prioritized, none of the work we do to serve others and maintain our home will count for anything.

Naomi's Baby Steps to Balance

When Naomi Marks joined Convivial Circle[3], her biggest ambition was simply to not have Cheerios on the floor all the time. With seven kids and an eighth on the way, everything felt like a disaster. For the first part of their marriage, Naomi and her husband moved about once a year while also adding babies on the regular. No wonder it felt hard.

The first and most important shift Naomi made was to change the way she thought about and talked about her life and her duties. Instead of thinking or saying, "My kids are just trying to make my life harder," she reminded herself that the job of a mom is caring for children. Children need care, and that's why she's there.

She identified another wrong story she'd fall into. She realized she was thinking of her home as a dollhouse. She wanted to be able to arrange the things and the people and have them stay put. Neither children nor things ever

3 See Appendix A.

stayed put, so not only was there work to do, but she felt an accompanying sense of failure and frustration. However, erasing the wrong story—not erasing the work—was her key to finding relief from discouragement.

Overwhelm, Naomi discovered, is a feeling and a choice. She said, "I can choose to not feel overwhelmed, and I can choose a different story. But this life is what God gave me, so I must be able to do it in Him."[4]

One of the first baby steps Naomi took was building the habit of never going to bed with dishes in the sink. This change alone made her feel more on top of her life and home. From there, she pulled out of a negative spiral and moved into a positive spiral as she recognized she could make use of five minutes here and there to make significant progress.

Naomi began the transformation of her attitude and the story in her head by writing alignment cards and placing them on her desk and in her kitchen. Some of Naomi's favorite alignment quotes are, "I have enough time to do the will of God," "Be an observer and experimenter, not an Eeyore," and "Just get up and make dinner."

Making dinner, she realized, was always an option she could choose instead of morosely sitting and thinking about how hard everything was. Getting up and doing something, even something small and basic, helped her climb out of her discouragement.

---

4 "A Total Home Life Makeover - with Pastor's wife Naomi Marks." Simplified Organization Podcast. December 2, 2022.

By doing fifteen minutes of organizing at a time, twenty times a month, Naomi actually got ahead of housekeeping in a way she never had when she thought of it as a single, all-encompassing project. She was about to go through every drawer, every closet, every room in just half a year.

Cleaning, decluttering, and organizing in fifteen-minute chunks here and there was completely painless, Naomi found, even while homeschooling, having babies, and being a pastor's wife. Now that she's been able to tackle her work head-on in small bites and see traction, she no longer despairs when she notices something has gotten out of hand. Now she knows how to deal with it. She knows she *will* deal with it. Embracing her work at home has taught her how to enjoy not only the work, but also her people more and more, because she no longer views them as walking undo buttons.

When she finished Simplified Organization Community Coaching, Naomi said, "This has changed my life completely. I can't believe someone with as many kids as I have in as big a house as I have can feel and be as organized as I am. My mom came to visit last week, and she always used to make comments about my 'messy house, happy kids,' but this time she commented that my house was so organized and clean."[5]

> *Therefore, as you received Christ Jesus the Lord, so walk in him, rooted and built up in him and established in the faith, just as you were taught, abounding in thanksgiving.*
>
> —Colossians 2:6–7

---

5 Ibid.

16

Gratitude Is the Best Motivation

Motivation isn't caused by a prod or goad, but by gratitude and faith

Gratitude bestows reverence, allowing us to encounter everyday epiphanies, those transcendent moments of awe that change forever how we experience life and the world.

—John Milton

Not only did the milk spill that morning, but the glass also fractured into a thousand pieces across the tile floor. Four small children were practicing self-sufficiency, and it didn't appear to be going very well.

With even more mess to clean than I'd been planning on, I heaved a grumpy sigh and grabbed a towel. I wondered what I was doing wrong. What should I teach them to prevent such mishaps? How should I admonish them so they'd be more careful?

As I was grouching in my mind and feigning patience on the outside, the Holy Spirit interrupted me with Scripture: "Let every person be quick to hear, slow to speak, slow to anger; for the anger of man does not produce the righteousness of God" (James 1:19–20).

But look at me! I'm not speaking! I'm keeping my mouth shut and not even griping at the kids about their muddle and the fact that they're causing me more work.

What about being slow to anger? What about the fact that I'm quick to fill my mental airtime with self-talk all about how this morning is already going all wrong? Could I be slow to speak even within myself about this situation?

Despite the Spirit's poking, I kept arguing. *I'm not yelling, so I don't think it counts as anger. It's just frustration. I'm just irritated. Not angry.*

Of course, these words are listed in the thesaurus under "anger." Was my irritation and frustration making things better or worse? If my responses weren't producing the righteousness of God, then wasn't *something* wrong with them?

Another Scripture filled my mind: "And we know that for those who love God all things work together for good, for those who are called according to his purpose" (Rom. 8:28). Even spilled milk and broken glass on my floor was not merely a neutral event, but something God was using for my good. How could that be? Is spilled milk ever *good*?

It *can* be good because the point is not the milk but the people affected by the milk. For my children, the milk spilled down their throats builds their bones and gives them energy for the day. For me that day, the milk spilled on the floor was an occasion for the Spirit to work in my heart.

Next up in the Spirit's conviction queue came a selection from the Heidelberg catechism we'd been memorizing: "All things, in fact, come to us not by chance but by his fatherly hand" (QA 27). Although it was a child's accident, the spill was not cosmically accidental. God used that spill so I'd stop and clean it up and have my pity-party exposed and cleaned up. I had a bigger mess than the milk that I might never have seen. The real clean-up job was happening inside my heart and mind.

Who Stole My Motivation?

It is easy and oh-so-common to feel unsuccessful as a homemaker and mother. We start out with high hopes and grand plans, only to be crushed by the weight of the daily reality of mundane duties. We feel defeated because our expectations are unreasonable. We imagine great works of charity and mercy that don't seem to fit our humdrum days. This is all the truer if we've bought into the magazine version of a successful, beautiful, organized home.

Why do we do what we do? The driving force behind our actions is *motivation*. Perhaps we lack motivation because we don't see the reason for the work. Sometimes, the action taken or the result achieved look the same even though the motivations are opposites. Which is more important—the action, the result, or the motivation?

We might be cleaning our kitchen to impress guests. Our motivation is to look good, to appear other than we are, to have our guests think highly of us. We clean because we are thinking of what others might think or say of us.

We might be cleaning our kitchen to keep up our pride. Our motivation is to be the best housekeeper, to be in control of our home, to have a beautiful home. We clean because we think highly of ourselves.

We might be cleaning our kitchen out of guilt. Our motivation is to be worthy of a kitchen upgrade, to show our mothers that we aren't poor excuses for homemakers, to demonstrate to our husbands that we do accomplish *something* during the day. We clean because we feel bad when we don't.

We might be cleaning our kitchen grudgingly, hating every minute of it. Our motivation is bare necessity, and we are bitter about it. We clean merely because, for one reason or another, we must.

Or, we might be cleaning our kitchen out of gratitude. Our motivation is love for our family, gratefulness for the gift of said kitchen, and anticipation of the service yet to be accomplished in it. As we clean, we notice blessing upon blessing surrounding us. Noticing blessing is encouraging; it's a spur, a reward.

Five different stories, all with the same outcome: a clean kitchen. Yet only one of them is a good story. Only one of them is the story we should be telling with our lives. In only one story do the motivation and action work together harmoniously.

If we find ourselves unmotivated to do the right thing, it is an indication that we either do not see how the task aligns with and moves us toward our purpose, or we have some alternate personal purpose like making life as easy and comfortable as possible. To glorify God is an all-encompassing purpose that gives significance to even the most mundane bits of life as well as its worst trials and sufferings.

We need to keep our purpose fixed before us. We clean because we are gladly, cheerfully fulfilling the duty set before us. We clean because God has cleaned us, and we are continuing to work that cleansing from our inner being out into our world. We clean because we are people made clean, no longer unclean.

We'll either attempt to become more organized for God's glory, grounded in gratitude, or for our own. Gratitude is God-centeredness and self-forgetfulness that works itself out in visible ways in our lives. It is demonstrated by action. Gratitude motivates and brings about action.

Gratitude Produces Fruitfulness

The Heidelberg catechism says that "Prayer is the most important part of the thankfulness God requires of us." Gratitude is to characterize our prayers as well as motivate them. We are told to pray with thankfulness even when we're making petitions:

> *Do not be anxious about anything, but in everything by prayer and supplication with thanksgiving let your requests be made known to God. And the peace of God, which surpasses all understanding, will guard your hearts and your minds in Christ Jesus.*
>
> —Phil. 4:6–7

The peace God promises is for those whose requests are accompanied by thanksgiving. Anxiety and worry are attitudes we need to flee. Peace and joy are fruit of the Holy Spirit, the attitudes of Christ we are to put on. God's peace, by the Holy Spirit, guards our heart, changes our attitudes, when we pray with thanksgiving.

Writing gratitude lists alone is not necessarily being grateful. Gratitude is more than a feeling in our heart. Our gratitude is meant to be aimed at God directly in prayer. All our prayer should be filled with thanksgiving, and all our gratitude should be directed into prayer.

Gratitude is the most potent motivator of love and good works, but gratitude isn't a shallow list of nice things you noticed. The gratitude we are called to is thanking God for His care and provision in the hard things, in real life, in all circumstances.

Working for God's glory rather than our own means we aren't doing our duty to earn points, to buy favor, or to get the outcome we want. It means we look at how we can obey God here and now rather than how we can wrestle Him into making others recognize our worth or even into making our children "turn out."

Instead, we ask Him to help us be faithful, and we trust He will use us, our efforts, and our children to tell a story in the world that glorifies Him in the end. He will do that, and it will be messy along the way. He promises us it will all work for our good in the end, not that He has a formula we can follow to get an easy life or a comfortable story. Thus, we can be grateful.

This perspective changes how we see our daily tasks as well as our long-term vision and goals. When this happens, we are walking humbly with our God, and our children and our community are affected at a much more fundamental level by our example than by our trying to micromanage their walks. As we watch God work, our gratitude increases.

Learning to make the right choice right now is learning wisdom. It is hard but worth it. Each time we choose to do what we know is right, instead of what gratifies our appetite or our laziness, is a step of faithfulness that God blesses with His grace, giving us the strength to carry on.

What if the purpose of our homemaking was not to have an organized house that is always clean, but to be a means of abounding in the work of the Lord? Then, when the work is abounding, we can be grateful that the mission is underway, rather than sad that we are not always at ease.

God Gives and Receives Gratitude

The story of a good and grateful life does not go, "She was so grateful that she napped, read, and took it easy." The thanksgiving God produces in us and we direct back to

Him is not simply a feeling; it is a motivator, a mover-and-shaker.

Thanksgiving does not merely well up in our hearts and make us feel warm and cozy. Because God gave, so we give. Because God cleanses, so we do, too. Because God loves, we love as well. It is duty and obedience, but it is also joyful imitation. In Christ, we are free from fear, pride, guilt, and bitterness. We are free to serve with joy.

We all know gratitude is important. But sometimes thankfulness seems a bit vague. Is gratitude a feeling we're supposed to float around in all day? A sentiment just bubbling up from our heart to our head and staying there, providing serene thoughts and a calm demeanor?

Do we just list out what we're grateful for in a journal, directing our thanksgiving to ourselves? Is that really thanksgiving or just a warm and fuzzy feeling? Are we expanding our gratitude muscle or are we merely listing things we like? Gratitude isn't gratitude unless it is directed at a person.

You can't be grateful to the world in general, to the universe or fate. The universe doesn't care. It is not a receiver of thanks. Gratitude is not a mere feeling nor simply positive thoughts. Thankfulness must be expressed for particular things to particular people. The Creator of the universe is a Person. He can be thanked, and He should be.

Gratitude overflowing in our hearts needs direction and expression, and our Creator is the proper recipient. A renewed heart and will produces a thankfulness that works itself out in our lives and affects not only what we do, but also how we do it. Let us show our gratitude to God for our family by smiling at them, even when they break our dishes and get in our way.

Gratitude is the antidote to the bad stories we tell ourselves about others, about ourselves, and about our work. When you find yourself spiraling into a pity-party, pull out by thanking God for what He is doing in that very situation. Let us show our gratitude for our homes by taking good care of them. Let us show our gratitude for our salvation by working it out with prayer and joy.

Growing in gratitude is not simply about feeling good feelings or listing things we enjoy, but about paying attention to God's hand in each situation and walking in faith. Gratitude is a concrete practice of trust and belief in God's goodness and a practice of kindness to others.

The more we learn to express gratitude to God in each and every situation, the more we see His hand at work, even in trials and hardships. The more we express gratitude to the people around us, the more it becomes contagious—a way of being, a way of interacting with one another in our homes.

Sing Your Way to Gratitude

Whenever we feel self-pity creep in, resentment rise, or frustration increase, we can pause, recognizing the self-centeredness of such emotions. We can put them to death by replacing them with gratitude to God. Gratitude, especially when put to melody, banishes our bad attitudes and guards our hearts from its attacks.

I have found that the best way to chase away a bad attitude is to sing. This tip works for kids and moms alike. When you're grumpy, you can't sing. If you start to sing anyway, your mind and heart are instantly affected by both the music and the words.

Next time you need an attitude adjustment, sing one of the hymns you've learned with your kids. Next time you need to stop the internal complaining about your work, turn on a peppy song and sing while you work.

God has given us a shortcut, a cheat code, to aligning our hearts and minds with truth by giving us the ability for and appreciation of music. We honor Him when we use it. National anthems, military marches, worship music—all the historic, effective uses of music remind us: Music is for more than pleasure and enjoyment. Music is a weapon, a shield, a uniting bulwark. Try it and see.

Gracie's Baby Steps to Grateful Traction

Gracie Madgwick was at a rough point, mentally and emotionally, when she joined Convivial Circle and started Simplified Organization Community Coaching[6]. She was often overwhelmed, living daily with mental turmoil and discouragement piling up. She had just had her seventh child, and she knew she needed to get a handle on her life, but she didn't know where to start.

---

6 See Appendix A.

She felt like she already didn't have enough time to do what she ought, so how could she take the time to plan? Worse, however, was the fact that she was not dwelling on truth, gratitude, and trust in her situation.

She began by recognizing what she was telling herself about her life. She needed the reminder to adjust her attitude, but she also needed to be given tools to start implementing life management practices. As soon as she shifted her attention to the truth about her situation, she began to see huge personal growth.

She says that her new management strategy boils down to just writing stuff down. Write it down, get it out of your head. Holding too much in your brain contributes to feeling overwhelmed and stuck. After embracing the habit of writing things down, Gracie noticed that she became a better problem-solver. Ideas and solutions came to her. She said, "The overwhelm really is in our heads. We have to clear our heads to get over it."[7]

Writing things down gives you that outside-of-yourself perspective to see what's going on, to celebrate progress you hadn't noticed, and to take the next step of faithfulness. Every checkmark is a mini-celebration, and Gracie learned to embrace thinking of them that way.

When she'd get partway into her morning and feel like she hadn't done anything, she'd look at her dashboard and realize she could check some things off. She became

---

7 "A Total Life Makeover Begins with Small Steps - with Gracie Madgwick." Simplified Organization Podcast. December 13, 2022.

thankful for her plan and began to notice what she was accomplishing with a spirit of gratitude. Her motivation and traction increased.

Gracie admitted that it can be overwhelming initially to start writing things down. You're not sure if it'll help or if you'll just be more overwhelmed when you see all that data on paper. She said, "I think the answer is that it does help. It has helped me a lot."

A weekly review might seem like a big deal, like it would take a lot of time, but Gracie has found it best if she keeps it simple and takes only twenty or so minutes. It doesn't have to be an hour or more. If you're doing it regularly, it can be a big blessing.

Gracie noticed that as she implemented new practices in any area of life, it was hard to see her own growth. Growth is slow. It's not overnight. It's hard to analyze where it's occurred. That's why outside input was very helpful, especially from her husband. She learned to stop when she felt discouraged and ask him if he was seeing progress. He would express his thankfulness and appreciation for her, and then she could move forward with mirrored gratitude.

> *Give thanks in all circumstances; for this is the will of God in Christ Jesus for you.*
>
> —1 Thessalonians 5:18

17

Smile and Start

Starting is the hardest part, but we can start small and start with a smile

A compassionate open home is part of Christian responsibility, and should be practiced up to the level of capacity.

—Francis Schaeffer, *True Spirituality: How to Live for Jesus Moment by Moment*

There was a time when "smile" was the top item on my daily to-do list. I could only pick three things to put on that daily card as priorities. Smile was No. 1 for weeks—because that's what I needed to focus on.

It was more important for me to visibly demonstrate I was happy to be where I was—with my children—to my children than it was to run a load of laundry or clean out the fridge.

Even though a homemaker was exactly what I wanted to be, even though I enjoyed the challenge of juggling mothering, meals, housework, and other projects I took on, I realized that what my children saw was not a mom who loved her life but a mom with a furrowed brow. No one could blame them if they thought mom was unhappy with her lot. My thinking face looked like disapproval, which was not how I wanted my kids to remember me.

Thus, tasks were displaced on my daily card by an admonition. I wanted to look up and smile when a child entered the room. I wanted to listen with a cheerful demeanor when we spoke. I wanted them to happen upon a happy mom when they saw me. Smiling at them was on the same level as cooking dinner for them. One nourished their spirits while the other nourished their bodies.

But smiling more benefitted me as well. I wouldn't have said before that I was unhappy, but after intentionally smiling more, I also *felt* happier. Each smile was a personal reminder that despite the work, I *was* happy. Perhaps, I even began to admit, the work itself was invigorating—as long as I approached it with vigor rather than languor. Smiling helped me start.

Just Start

"Smile and start" is one of my favorite mottos. It smashes together the two things that I think are most important in home management: smiling and starting.

Sometimes a bad mood is brought on by our own underlying procrastination. We don't want to, so we don't, then we feel worse because we aren't. We have to cut the cycle short by starting, even if we don't feel like it, because we realize the feeling will follow.

We get stuck spinning our wheels because we think we don't know what to do, especially when there's too much to do. The only way to get unstuck is to smile, which will help you switch out of panic mode.

Smiling disarms the stress that so easily mounts. Stress is bad for our health, for our minds, for our kids. The only way to reject the stress response is to acknowledge we are not in control, but God is, and we can trust Him. In that, we can always find a smile of gratitude.

Get unstuck by starting—by taking action on one small, simple thing right in front of you. The path will be made clear as you smile and start.

Choose to Smile

It seems so basic, yet it takes work to make a smile our default. Our heavenly Father is pleased with us and pleased when we come to Him. He is our role model for parenting. This earthly mother tends to enter a room, cast a critical eye about, and be generally dissatisfied with what she sees.

Even if we're not dissatisfied with the children themselves, they pick up and internalize whatever vibe we emit. If we marinate in thoughts like, "Things aren't very good around here right now," they will feel that burden personally, even if they can't express it.

It is a simple, logical step to deduce that when Mom is grumpy because of the smudges on the walls and windows, the scattered books and toys, and the constant chatter, it is the children who make her grumpy. After all, those irritants would not be there if the children were not there.

It seems crazy that it is so hard to do such a simple thing, but it is a fallen world. Good and right are not our natural defaults. But with God's strength and the Holy Spirit's help (He does grant self-control and love and patience when honestly petitioned), it is our calling and a duty we can fulfill.

We can choose to smile on demand. Consciously choose the emotions you display, and the outward act of the will can work its way inward to change our emotions. If we find ourselves in need of a little attitude organization, one simple step we can take is to breathe deeply, then smile. Organizing our attitude is something we must continually do, and smiling is a simple tactic we can make use of that is good for us and our family.

Love Is Communicated by a Smile

Smiling is the overlooked secret to a happy home. Mom looking into her children's eyes and smiling at them is a tangible, easy way to make them feel loved. A wife smiling as her husband walks through the door sets a tone of love and comfort. When you aren't sure what to do, smile at your people.

> When you aren't sure what to do, smile at your people.

I know it's embarrassing to put "smile" on your to-do list, but it really is important enough to prioritize in this way if it's not a natural instinct. It's a worthwhile habit to invest in, even if it means eating some humble pie and taking up a slot in our daily top three. Smiling comes naturally to some and less easily to others, but it is a simple gesture that can steer us clear of negativity.

When we have "smile" on our to-do list instead of some project-oriented task, we're reminded that it's not all about getting things done. Our real job is to invest in people, and smiling at them is an important way to do that. Smiling is contagious for our children. They will catch and mimic what we model, so we should be conscious of our expressions.

All people, children included, want to be heard, seen, known, valued. Our children's pestering chatter is often a sign that they aren't getting what they know they need: attention. And they will keep knocking, knocking, knocking until they get it, or they despair. Smiling is a simple first step to giving them what they are seeking. Both smiling by default and looking them in the eye are ways of giving attention, of really looking and seeing, to communicate that we want them, love them, and know them.

Kristin's Baby Steps to Smile and Start

Kristin Ching came into the Convivial Circle community[8] after researching productivity principles for stay-at-home moms.[9] She was expecting her eighth child when she started Simplified Organization Community Coaching, but she jumped in because she wanted help getting back on track after baby.

---

8 See Appendix A

9 Kristin also writes about Christian motherhood at lovejinthesmallthings.com

At the time, she felt frazzled and easily upset with her children, but she knew the problem was her own heart and not the kids. Struggling with perfectionism, she needed the constant reminder that she wasn't supposed to be in control of everything. She was just supposed to serve effectively where God had called her—in her home, with her family.

She started with brain dumps and a weekly overview planning sheet. Whenever she began to feel overwhelmed, she recognized it not only as a temptation, but also as an opportunity to choose faith instead of control. She'd write out her thoughts longhand, gaining perspective by taking her concerns to the Lord in prayer. After using brain dumps and prayer to calm down, she'd decide what was most important to work on first and just get started.

Because she has so much written down, she now looks back over her weeks, months, and years and sees how much God has given her to accomplish, how much God has taught her, and how much God has blessed her. Instead of only giving thanks for happy things, she began truly giving thanks in everything, which helped her smile at her children more and more genuinely.

As she smiled at her children more, giving thanks in all things, she stressed less about their messes. She was able to regulate her attitude with the help of the Holy Spirit, and her sanctification affected everything else in their home. Instead of working toward achieving a clean house, she saw her work as simply getting the props set up for the next scene in their life.

Although she didn't finish every task on her list or the Community Coaching checklist, she recognized and rejected the temptation of perfectionism. In the long run, just continuing on the path, even though the systems weren't perfect, would pay off—and it did. Kristin saw improvement not only in her own approach, but also across the board in her home. It wasn't perfect. It wasn't smooth and easy. But it was growth and progress.

"Sometimes," she said, "I just have to be persistent even when I can't be completely consistent." Consistency is more about achieving sameness of outcome with sameness, of effort, but that's not generally how life works. On the other hand, persistence is continuing in our efforts even when it is difficult. Kristin is right. We need persistence more than we need consistency.

Next Comes the Race

Today is the day. There is no single leaf to turn over and start fresh, no simple solution or quick fix. There is no magic formula or secret sauce. There is only waking up each day and doing what we can, where we are, in faithful responsibility.

We want something we can check off and be done with, but that's simply not the nature of housework. The fact that housework won't be done in this life does not need to discourage us. Instead, we can choose to practice, to make progress, and give up on our false hopes of being "done."

The goal isn't a perfectly clean and put-together home. The goal is making our resources useful and available for building up people. This means those large housework projects don't need to be complete for you to be faithful in your work. The room doesn't have to stay clean for it to be worth your time.

Just baby step toward progress, because there will always be the need for small steps. Getting organized is only the preliminary work, after all, not the real work. That doesn't make it unimportant or a waste of time, but it does mean that we can't sigh, sit back, and think we've done the hard part once we have our lists in order. Having our stuff in order is only getting us to the starting line with running shoes and a water bottle. Next comes the actual race.

Let's smile and start.

> *Strength and dignity are her clothing, and she laughs at the time to come. She opens her mouth with wisdom, and the teaching of kindness is on her tongue. She looks well to the ways of her household and does not eat the bread of idleness. Her children rise up and call her blessed; her husband also, and he praises her: "Many women have done excellently, but you surpass them all." Charm is deceitful, and beauty is vain, but a woman who fears the LORD is to be praised. Give her of the fruit of her hands, and let her works praise her in the gates.*
>
> —Proverbs 31:25–31

Acknowledgments

The skeleton of what became Simplified Organization started as a postpartum brain dump when I was in my late twenties. I didn't want things to slip back to the level of chaos and mismanagement I had orchestrated my first six or so years of motherhood. I made a list for myself of what I needed to get a grip on in my home and routines. Instead of expecting to knock it all out in a week, I sketched it out over three months—my first version of accepting that baby steps were required.

A couple of years later, I made another version for another postpartum season, and I thought maybe it might be helpful to others. Others didn't need my checklist, but we all need help processing our own lives and figuring out what we should actually be tackling. So I drew up a plan for working through various areas of homemaking, with a what-and-how approach for women to make their own "home recovery plan."

Over the last decade, the Simplified Organization eCourse has gone through several major overhauls and many revisions and iterations. Each time, it's been developed based not only on my own experience, but on working through it with dozens and then hundreds of others who offer their own insights, who tell me where my thoughts are muddy, and who have been great encouragements to me in sticking with this program.

To the many people who told me it needed to be a book, thank you for pestering. Here you go. To the many women who stuck with me through all the different revisions and platform changes, thank you so much. Thank you to Stefani Mons and Virginia Lee Rogers, who edited the last revision of the courses. Thank you to Harmony Harkema for editing this manuscript, making sure it didn't read like a blog post anthology, and to Melinda Martin for making the design fun and beautiful.

When it comes to sticking it out with me, my husband and kids take the cake. We are a team where each member sees that we can all be better about doing—anything, everything. I pray the net effect is that we've all spurred one another on to love and good works, and I praise God for our fellowship with one another. Thanks for years of EHAPing and clean teams, for putting up with laundry and meal highs and lows, and for your good-natured humor. Most of all, thank you, Matt, for always bringing the truth to me in love.

My testimony is one of God never letting me get far before returning me to His Word and being convicted therein. Prone to wander, Lord, I feel it, yet there You always are. The Spirit has also brought conviction and instruction to me through the work of Elisabeth Elliot, Rachel Jankovic, Doug and Nancy Wilson, Leila Lawler, Francis and Edith Schaeffer, and the Heidelberg Catechism. If this work of mine contributes anything to others' journeys in sanctification, then I praise the Lord's ability to draw straight with crooked lines, as Pastor Doug says.

May the Lord bless this book to your heart and home so that you, your home, and your family are bright, shining testimonies to the reality of True Truth, to the potency of the gospel, in a world that needs it so very badly. Don't forget your own duty to pass on your hard-won wisdom and mercy-shaped story to the younger women God puts in your path. Titus 2 is a call for all of us. Let us live it out, that the word of God may not be reviled. After all, it is God Who will make good on that Word. Let's trust and obey.

> *Now may the God of peace who brought again from the dead our Lord Jesus, the great shepherd of the sheep, by the blood of the eternal covenant, equip you with everything good that you may do his will, working in us that which is pleasing in his sight, through Jesus Christ, to whom be glory forever and ever. Amen.*
>
> —Hebrews 13:20–21

ABOUT THE AUTHOR

Mystie Winckler

Mystie Winckler married her high school sweetheart, Matt, at nineteen; together they have five children they educated at home. Their oldest son is married, their second son is in college, and three are still at home, keeping life fun and interesting. The Wincklers live in Moscow, Idaho, and love extending hospitality together.

When she's not cooking, teaching, reading, or cleaning, Mystie publishes articles, podcast episodes, and videos about cheerful, competent homemaking and homeschooling on her website, SimplyConvivial.com. Her community, Convivial Circle, is a treasure trove of mother-mentors engaged in the work at home to which they've been called.

Mystie is also a cohost of Scholé Sisters, a podcast for classical homeschooling moms who are educating themselves while educating their kids.

Whether talking about personal lives, homemaking duties, or homeschooling days, Mystie seeks to return to and live out the motto, *Repent. Rejoice. Repeat.*

Appendix A

Find Accountability with Convivial Circle

Do any of these sound familiar?

- ☐ You constantly feel the pressure of having too much to do, so you grab your phone and open Facebook, just to stop the internal nagging of your own mind.
- ☐ You know there's no getting to the end of the to-do list, so it's hard even to start.
- ☐ The work never seems to end. There's always more to do, no job is ever complete, and whatever you do is quickly undone by other people.
- ☐ You keep trying to get to a base-level "square one" so you can move forward. But you can't make it.
- ☐ You're so overwhelmed, you don't even know what to do first.
- ☐ You feel stuck.

You can find fulfillment *and* joy in your home.

Get the progress and peace you've been looking for with courses, mentorship calls, accountability, and more to keep you gospel-focused and motivated in the mundane.

I don't know about you, but I went into this homemaking and mothering gig thinking it would be easy. "It's just laundry and dishes. How hard could it be?"

It turns out, pretty hard.

It turns out that what makes you a good kid, a good student, or a good employee will not make you a good homemaker. But no one tells you this stuff.

Homemaking isn't easy or obvious. God told older women to teach younger women because we all need mentors.

Most people seem to think that paying jobs need training, but keeping the house is work for the unskilled. Either that or it's so negligible it can be done on the side after "more important things"—like a career.

As Christian women, we know that managing family and home life is our calling, whether we also have paid work or not. Homemaking is a primary way we serve God.

But no one is around to teach us how.

Convivial Circle is where you'll find both instruction and mentoring so you can be a homemaker who glorifies God. With weekly seminars, Zoom meetups, private chat groups, accountability, and over a dozen courses, we want you to be equipped to be an effective, cheerful homemaker with a deep and broad capacity to glorify God where He has called you.

"I definitely struggle with a boom-and-bust cycle, and the overwhelm that always happens after the bust. I always want to completely overhaul things. I think iterating is the best lesson I have learned from Mystie. Now my mindset is much better around planning and making progress step-by-step. There is no perfect plan. I have far more grace for myself and am seeing real and lasting improvement in my home and in how I feel about life."

—Elizabeth DeLoach,
homeschooling mom and pastor's wife

"Convivial Circle has been a lifeline. Your ideas are so thorough and practical, but I've never before worked through something like this that led to worship of God. Thank you for not skirting the most important areas and deeper issues. You are mentoring me on the other side of the world, and I thank you from the bottom of my heart for sharing such solid work and deep honesty."

—Sarah Arnold,
mom and overseas missionary

Go to
simplyconvivial.com/stop-overwhelm
to learn more.

Appendix B

The Simplified Organization Action Plan

Visit simplifiedorganization.com to get a printable checklist version of this action plan.

Step 1: Tell true stories.

- Set a timer for five minutes and brain dump. Set a timer for another five minutes and pray about everything you spilled onto the paper. (Ch. 1)
- Copy a Bible verse you want to make the song of your heart and the focus of your thoughts onto an index card. Tape it to your bathroom mirror at eye level and pray it every time you stand there at the sink. (Ch. 7)

Step 2: Tame your inner toddler.

- As you build new and better habits, watch and replace all grumbling, dismissing, and self-sympathy with three seconds of appreciating the good effect you've had on your environment. (Ch. 3)

- Give your routines or tedious tasks an amusing, catchy name and use it a lot. Want the kids to wipe out the sink after they brush their teeth? Want to do that yourself? Call it "Spit and Shine." Need to just start folding laundry already, but you're always reluctant? Call it "Learning with Laundry" and listen to a podcast or an online course or an audiobook while you fold. (Ch. 8)

Step 3: Take baby steps

- Choose one small area of your house that bothers you or that you've been procrastinating working on. Set a timer for ten minutes and simply do what you can in that time, then stop when the timer goes off. (Ch. 2)
- Choose three important things that must be done today. Write the date and day of the week at the top of a post it or index card, then list your top three for today. Try again tomorrow. (Ch. 9)

Step 4: Invest your time

- Take a picture of your kitchen. Spend five minutes—with a timer—tidying things up and cleaning. Take another picture after the five minutes. Notice the difference you were able to make in such a short time. (Ch. 5)
- Spend fifteen minutes preparing yourself for the coming week. During your fifteen-minute weekly review, look over your calendar for the next two weeks, taking notes about how best to prepare for what's ahead. Prepare a fresh routine checklist and task list for the next week, moving over the things that didn't happen last week. Take some notes about meals or groceries based on your activities this week, even if it's not a complete menu plan. Set a timer and remember that some is better than none. (Ch. 10)

Step 5: Establish small routines

- Pick one small surface and remove the things that don't belong there. If you can, put them away quickly; otherwise, just put them in a temporary holding place. Wipe the surface and arrange the remaining items neatly. Take a moment to appreciate the order you've created. (Ch. 4)

- Before dinner, call the kids and spend fifteen minutes—with a timer, all together—EHAPing: putting things away in their own home. Turn on music and make it a cheerful team effort. No matter how far you get, celebrate and be done when the timer goes off. Try it again tomorrow. (Ch. 11)

Step 6: Pursue hospitality

- As the mother setting the tone of the home, building the family, one of the most productive things you can do is smile more at your people. Your cheerful, loving demeanor builds people, builds cultures, and builds your own work ethic. (Ch. 6)
- Remember that the child you're upset with today will be an adult guest in your home before you know it. The way you relate now is laying the groundwork for your relationship then. Ask your child's forgiveness whenever you sin against him. (Ch. 12)

Made in the USA
Monee, IL
04 February 2024

52479057R00152